TABLE OF CONTENTS

I0877577

Cyclical Learning Processes in Second Language Production

Werkstattreihe Deutsch als Fremdsprache

Herausgegeben von
Rolf Ehnert, Bielefeld
und
Rolf Klemmt, Jyväskylä
Donatella Ponti-Dompé, Turin
Muneshige Hosaka, Mito

Band 10

Verlag Peter Lang
Frankfurt am Main · Bern · New York · Nancy

Mary Carroll

Cyclical Learning Processes in Second Language Production

Verlag Peter Lang
Frankfurt am Main · Bern · New York · Nancy

CIP-Kurztitelaufnahme der Deutschen Bibliothek

Carroll, Mary:

Cyclical learning processes in second language production / Mary Carroll. - Frankfurt am Main ; Bern ; New York ; Nancy : Lang, 1984.
(Werkstattreihe Deutsch als Fremdsprache ; Bd. 10)
ISBN 3-8204-7341-6
NE: GT

ISSN 0721-4278
ISBN 3-8204-7341-6
© Verlag Peter Lang GmbH, Frankfurt am Main 1984

Alle Rechte vorbehalten.
Nachdruck oder Vervielfältigung, auch auszugsweise, in allen Formen wie Mikrofilm, Xerographie, Mikrofiche, Mikrocard, Offset verboten.
Druck und Bindung: Weihert-Druck GmbH, Darmstadt

1. INTRODUCTION

Learning a language is a cognitive, social and linguistic activity and we learn and produce language for the purpose of communicating with others. During language acquisition learners are not primarily engaged in inducing a certain system from a particular set of data but are first and foremost concerned with communicating as effectively as possible with the means at their disposal.
While a large body of research in the late sixties and early seventies was devoted to the description of structural features of the learner's output and the factors which encourage or impede attainment of target-like proficiency, the late seventies were characterized by a shift in focus to a functional perspective of the learner's behaviour and to how learner languages function in communication as systems in their own right. Acquisition involves more than hypothesis testing and revision; the way learners make use of their resources in communication relates to the course the learning process takes. In second language learning in particular, the degree of communicative success achieved rather than conformity with features of the target system may determine whether forms are abandoned or retained during the learning process.

Research into language learning aims at discovering how language acquisition[1] proceeds, how the learner language is structured at various points, how it is put to use in everyday interactions, and the factors which determine why it takes one course and not another. The present longitudinal study of the developing abilities of 5 English-speaking students of German at university level focuses on the development of their syntactic system, as evidenced in everyday conversational exchanges.

Learning the syntax of a language is often represented as the internalisation of a system of rules which is constantly revised or restructured as development proceeds. Ideally speaking replacement will occur when existing rules fail to serve communicative purposes efficiently or fail to account for some feature of the target language. Given the fact, however, that when using a language learners are faced with the problem of having to learn a task while performing it, constraints on the course acquisition takes can also be expected at the performance level.

[1] In the following language 'learning' and 'acquisition' are treated as synonyms.

As pointed out by J.B. Carroll (1971) and Levelt (1975) cognitive theories of human behaviour and learning have generally ignored the field of "human performance theory", i.e. the study of skills and attentional processes. Language learning within a cognitive framework describes learning as a process of hypothesis generation, testing and revision, i.e. as the acquisition of knowledge. However, "knowledge cannot explain performance (...) without recourse to additional principles of learning and behaviour organisation". (Levelt, 1975). In other words, we cannot study the structure of language without being concerned with the nature of the behaviour in which it is manifest. With the location of language use and learning within the framework of human performance theory, performance factors do not figure as distortive elements but as a constitutive part of language production and reception.

It is, as yet, unclear how limitations on processing and attentional capacities affect the process of acquisition. Language production, for example, involves the incorporation of knowledge from various sources and the integration of skills which, as with any other kind of performance, have to be practised before being mastered. Since learners, when using language, cannot devote unlimited attention to all aspects of the task in hand, the question remains as to how the problem of divided attention is dealt with in a way which ensures that communication is effected successfully and how this shapes the learning process, if at all.
These questions are confounded by the fact that the productive side of language behaviour provides the most accessible basis of observation from which inferences are made as to the principles governing the development process. In any language learning context the ability to understand language generally precedes the ability to produce it, so that discrepancies between both aspects of language behaviour may be considerable.

In this study the focus of interest is therefore not only on the point at which a particular structure is acquired but on how long it takes for it to become fully established and how it relates to other alternatives at various points in time - at least as evidenced in production. The relationships between successive phases of development fall into a wide range and involve revisions such as rule addition, rule loss, re-ordering and re-structuring etc., where addition and loss may be abrupt or gradual.
In order to assess the status of any form in a system at a given point in development it is necessary to evaluate the application of this form against

all relevant alternatives present - a procedure which involves the quantitative analysis of variation in application.[2] If this process of integration of new forms is not instantaneous, i.e. applying in all relevant contexts simultaneously and to the same degree, the course of development can be described on the basis of features - both linguistic and non-linguistic, which encourage or inhibit the learner's application of new forms. This constitutes the procedure of analysis applied in the following.

This work is a revised version of a doctoral dissertation presented at the University of Heidelberg, 1981. I would like to thank the following people for their encouragement and help: Rainer Dietrich, Herbert-Ernst Wiegand, Clive Perdue, Martha Carroll, Ann Kelly and David Godfrey.

---

[2] A procedure originating in sociolinguistic studies in variation (cf. Labov, 1969) and applied in second language learning (see Klein 1974, Dickerson 1976, Klein/Dittmar 1979).

2. DATA COLLECTION

Since what people say is usually relevant to the situation in which communication takes place the characteristics of a speech sample will be influenced by the nature of the situation in which it is recorded. The data-collection situation on which the following analysis is based cannot be said to be representative in that it leads to data which show a learner's range of control over many aspects of language at any point in development. The data represent only a slice of the learner's performance and the analysis is restricted to showing how their performance developed within a particular communicative framework which remained fairly constant over the period of observation. Furthermore, it was not possible within the framework of this study to carry out any observations as to the authenticity of their behaviour. The one divergence many of them remarked on between this data collection and other uses of German was that they normally did not hold forth so extensively "in bad German" on any topic. The implication being that there is a limit to the amount a native speaker can be expected to take!

The aim of this study is to trace how evolving systems are re-organised at the syntactic level during the process of acquisition. Although one can expect a good deal of individual variation, general principles of re-organisation, if present, may best be detected by pooling the data of learners — learners who have reached a comparable stage of development, who share a common learning situation — and charting their progress from one particular point onwards.

This chapter deals with the criteria under which the learners were selected, the data- collection situation, the frequency of the recording sessions and ends with a brief description of the learners given in tabular form. Since language development is a continuous process it was decided to limit the number of informants to no more than five[3] so their rate of progress could be documented at sufficiently frequent intervals. The tape-recorded conversations were held with each learner individually. These conversations lasted approximately one hour and took place, as far as possible, every week for a period of nine weeks. The data base consisted, therefore, of an average of 5 hours/week of recorded speech, amounting to approximately forty hours in all.

[3]This number happened to be as many as could be managed per week.

2.1 The Selection of the Learners

The main requirements were that the learners should be at a comparable stage of development and could be expected to show progress over the limited period of observation available. The learners were attending German language classes at the University of Heidelberg which are designed to help students attain entry requirements to degree courses. All students attending these classes are required to take a Placement Test which rates both communicative as well as formal language skills. The members of this group of learners were placed at intermediate level on a scale ranging from "beginners", "intermediate" to "advanced". Since the term lasts approximately ten weeks and the majority of students leave afterwards for an extensive period, the span of any longitudinal study in this context is limited to this period. The third factor kept constant in addition to 'stage of development' and 'learning situation' was the source language. Although there is no clear evidence either way as to the role played by the source language in shaping subsequent learning processes, the group was confined to native speakers of English. As to other variables, any study of this type is dependent on volunteers and whether, after the initial selection, they have other factors in common - apart from their generosity - cannot be easily ascertained at the outset. As it turned out, four of the five who volunteered were outgoing and communicative, only one was reticent (Karin, see below) and inclined to focus attention on the formal correctness of utterances.
The development process was not traced from "beginners" level, i.e. from scratch, since there was not a sufficiently large group of learners with any one source language at that level. Secondly, and more importantly, beginners do not usually communicate at length so that the risk of obtaining insufficient data over a short period such as this is high.

2.2 The Encounters

The conversations were held with each learner individually and the same 'interviewer' conducted all the sessions. This type of situation is characterised by the fact that its central aim is to get the learner to communicate in her second language, and it is left to the 'interviewer' to create the appropriate atmosphere. The initial encounters consisted on the whole of question-answer exchanges where the 'interviewer' did most of the question-

ing. This pattern changed somewhat when the participants got to know each other better; conversations took a more 'natural' course with the learners often taking the initiative.
The learners were told at the outset that their conversations would be recorded[4] and analysed and that it would be preferable to withhold any further details until the end of the period of observation. They were also assured that if they then had any objections then their data would not be used.

The fact that the interviewer was also a native speaker of English did not seem to present a major problem. On the one hand this fact did not emerge until the second encounter, by which time German had been established as the language of communication. There was little code-switching or mixing and the learners always attempted to express themselves in German. This situation may be attributable to the fact that students from the US are generally inclined to avail of any opportunity of speaking German during their stay there and often speak German consistently amongst themselves. If they found the situation bizarre they did not, thankfully, let it affect their willingness to speak German.
The initial encounters were taken up with questions involving the informants' history. In the subsequent conversations the only strategy followed was to find topics which the learner was interested in and willing to enlarge upon spontaneously. Comparability across recording sessions was thus given at this level and not with respect to the topics treated.

The recordings generally took place in the afternoon or evening in a small study in the university buildings. Recordings in the learner's home proved to be a problem since they were mostly sharing rather confined quarters.

The following table gives a brief overview of the informants' social data. As shown in the section "previous tuition in German" two of the learners, Ieke and Karin, had taken German as a B.A. subject. The "intensive beginners course" (approx. 25 hours/week) refers to the course preceding the one the group was attending, and had taken place the previous term. 'High School' refers to three to four hours of tuition per week of the school year.

[4]The microphone was visible during each recording.

DATA ON THE INFORMANTS

Name	Nationality and Age	Previous Tuition in German	Knowledge of other languages	Contact with Germans	Attendance at language class	In Germany prior to observ. for:	Reason for learning German
Ieke	USA (21)	B.A. Subject, USA	Dutch	frequent	100%	3.5 months	B.A.
Joe	USA (21)	High School, USA	–	very frequent	0%	3.5 months	good knowledge of German
Karin	USA (21)	B.A. Subject, USA	Spanish (good)	frequent	100%	2,5 months	B.A.
Martha	IRL.(19)	intensive beginners course, FRG.	School French	frequent	60%	7 months	good knowledge of German
Rick	USA (24)	High School, USA	Spanish (good) School French	frequent	30%	1 year	knowledge of German

As the column 'attendance at language class' shows not all learners were exposed to the same learning situation. Joe, for instance, a medical student in the U.S.,gave up the classes after two or three days and decided to attend lectures in the medical faculty instead.

2.3 The Language Class

The main emphasis in this course is placed on vocabulary development and the overall improvement of communicative skills. A record was kept of the main grammatical items treated and their order of presentation during the first five weeks of the course. This record of the 'structure of the day' was not kept in order to assess the merits of formal tuition in this learning situation but was intended merely as a source of reference should this be required later during the analysis.

2.4 Data Selection and Transcription

Data selection was made in respect of the aim of the study - tracing the development and re-organisation of the learner's syntactic system. All utterances were transcribed and divided into sentences. Typical features of spoken speech were not recorded in detail; hesitations and self-corrections were only roughly marked. The analysis was based on passages where the learners spoke at length and with few interruptions, and did not encounter any major difficulties in expressing what they wished to convey. The analysis was then confined to syntactically complete sentences.

Four points of comparison were selected, the first at the end of the second week, the next after the fourth, then after week seven and finally after week nine. These points are referred to in the following as Phase I, II, III and IV.

Contributions from each learner in the pooled data amounted to at least 50 sentences each, giving a data set of approximately 250 sentences for each point of comparison. The following samples from the productions of three learners provide typical instances of the passages selected.

2.5 Text Samples[5]

(i) Ieke

/ Heute nachmittag meine zimmerkamaradin und ich treffen uns

this afternoon my roommate and I meet each other

[5]The symbol "+" refers to a short pause; (...) to interviewer passages; / to units analyzed as sentences or clauses.

bei der mensa / dann gehen wir weiter um ein fahhrad zu kaufen/
at the mensa then go we on in order a bicycle to buy

ich habe mich entschlossen/ dass ich soll wirklich nur deutsch
I have decided that I should really only german

sprechen/ es ist ganz schlimm/ ich konnte natürlich nicht
speak it is really bad I could naturally not

deutsch diese wochenende sprechen/ weil meine Verwandten
german this weekend speak because my relatives

verstehen es nicht/ Ich habe eine freundin mitgebracht/
understand it not I have a girl friend brought with me

und wir haben uns beide entschlossen/ dass wir reisen
and we have both decided that we travel

diese sommer zusammen/ ich glaube es geht/ diese wochenende
this summer together I think it works This weekend

haben wir zusammen gereist/ wir haben viel spass/ aber
have we together travelled, we had much fun but

wenn ich deutsch spreche/ dann spricht sie kein deutsch
when I german speak then speaks she no german

zurück/"bitte sprech kein deutsch hier"/weil für sie kein
back "please speak no german here" because for her no

problem/ sie kann schnell verwechseln zwischen deutsch und englisch/
problem she can quickly change between german and english

bei meiner verwandte ich habe einen Onkel der sehr gut
at my relatives I have an uncle who very well

deutsch sprechen können/und so wir haben deutsch mit ihm
german speak can and so we have german with him

gesprochen/und ich konnte gar nichts sagen/weil die
spoken and I could nothing at all say because the

Gwen hat alles gesagt / und ich stehe da stumm /
Gwen has everything said and I stand there - dumb

(dann hat mein + die verwandten ah du kannst
then has my + the relatives ah you can

aber gut deutsch sprechen zu Gwen) / ich kann es auch
really well german speak to Gwen I can it also

ein bisschen/aber sie sagten nicht darüber/weil als ich neben
a little but they said nothing about it because as I beside

ihr stand / dann bin ich schlecht
her stood then I am bad.

(ii) Martha

ich arbeite in Eppelheim/und ich muss abends arbeiten/
I work in Eppelheim and I must evenings work

manchmal arbeite ich zweimal in der woche/ (...)
sometimes work I twice in the week (....)

also ich setze mich dahin für drei stunden oder so /
right I seat (myself) down for three hours or so

und ich muss papier in jeder zeitung stellen / wir
and I must paper in every newspaper place. we

haben eine pause und manchmal musik /(......)
have a break and sometimes music (......)

ich kriege eine zeitung frei / aber es ist komisch /
I get a newspaper free but it is funny

ich kann nicht lesen/ die wörter sind so lang /
I can not read the words are so long

vielleicht ich kann ein satz verstehen/aber überall ich
perhaps I can a sentence understand but overall I

ich kann nicht / weil es nicht für kindern geschrieben
I can not because it not for children written

geschr .... / es ist nicht für kindern geschrieben /
writt .... it is not for children written (....)

ich habe in H. gewohnt / und es ist ganz neben der weg
I have in H. lived and it is (right) beside the road

wo + / ja und ungefähr um sechs oder halb sieben
where + 'yes and about at six or six-thirty

bin ich aufgewacht / weil es sind so viel autos draussen /
am I woke up because there are so many cars outside

und morgen abend muss ich auch noch arbeiten /
and tomorrow night must I also again work

(iii) Rick

als ich früher hier war / es hat mir gut gefallen die leute
as I earlier here was (I enjoyed it) the people

die stadt alles / jetzt ich finde es wie ein anderer
the town everything now I find it like (any) other

stadt / es ist gleich dieselbe als Los Angeles / es
town it is (just the same) as Los Angeles there

gibt kein unterschied zu viele leute zu viel probleme /
is no difference too many people too many problems

(....) meistens glaube ich es ist die leute / es gibt zu
(....) mostly think I it is the people there are too

viele polizisten / (die nachbarn sind immer) + / man kann
many policemen the neighbours are always + one can

nicht tun was er will / ich habe seit letzte jahr vier
not do what he wants I have since last year four

mal umgezogen / die nachbar kommen immer/ (klopfen an meine
times (moved flat) the neighbours come always bang on my

tür sagen du kannst das klavier nicht spielen)/heute
door say you can the piano not play today

ist ein feiertag/und du kannst spielen nicht/ich habe
is a holiday and you can play not I have

einen freund eingeladen zum frühstück/ das war gegen
a friend invited for breakfast that was about

acht uhr glaube ich/ und die nachbar ist ausgekommen
eight o'clock think I and the neighbour is come out

und sagte ruhe! ruhe/ wir können nicht schlafen/
and said be quiet we can not sleep

und ich glaube dass um acht das ist ein gute zeit
and I think that at eight that is a good time

zum frühstücken /
for breakfast

(iv) Joe

ich war gestern in KPD film gegangen/ es war ein
I was yesterday in KPD film gone it was a

propaganda film/ dann war ich zurück hier gekommen/
propaganda film then (was) I back here came

(und ich habe jemand) + / es gab ein mann der
and I have someone + there was a man who

Thomas heisst/(ein student ungefähr 24) und/er wird
is called Thomas a student about 24 and he will

ein lehrer sein / und ich sagte komm bei meiner wohnung/
a teacher be and I said come to my flat

wir werden ein bier trinken/ (und etwas reden) und/ ich
we will a beer drink and talk and I

sagte ich wohne bei einem corp jetzt/ er hat so viel
said I live in a fraternity now. he has so much

angst vor das corp/ und er hat schild erste mai/ of course
fear of the fraterninty and has badge May 1st " "

die leute sind keine echte reaktionär/politischerweise
the people are not real reactionaries politically

wir sind liberal/ - (keine kommunisten aber kein
we are liberal - not communists but not

reaktionär)
reactionary

3. DATA ANALYSIS

3.1 Probabilistic Grammars

The central characteristic of the learner's language system is that it is changing and not static. An adequate description of the learning process must show not only what changes occur as the learner progresses but also how transitions are effected, whether forms appear and disappear abruptly or are gradually phased out, and if changes are gradual, how these in fact proceed. It is therefore necessary to assess the use of each form against all possible alternatives present during various periods of development, comparing one phase with the next.

This can be carried out by writing a grammar which incorporates the complete set of rules describing all grammatical regularities found over different periods of development. The nature of the transitions can be described by probabilistically weighting all rules with respect to likelihood of application at successive points in time. In other words, this overall grammar describes all regularities of the learner system, and the transitons which mark specific features of development at various points in time are represented as changing probabilities of occurrence of rules.

This approach is based on the method proposed in Klein (1974) for describing variation in language.

The type of grammar suited to the description will depend on the objectives of the study and the nature of the data gathered. Phrase structure grammars are suited to the description of surface structure phenomena - the level of analysis in this study - and their properties are well documented in the literature. Designation of form/function relations did not prove problematic since this learner language is at an advanced stage of development - at the syntactic level at least.

In the following a brief description is given of the phrase structure grammar, of the way in which it was adapted to the needs of this analysis and, finally, of the procedure whereby rules were weighted. A detailed discussion of the variety grammar concept and the various problems associated with rule weighting can be found in Klein (1974, 1979).

A normal form context-free grammar consists of

1. a terminal vocabulary V_t
2. an auxiliary vocabulary V_n where $V_n \cap V_t = \emptyset$, i.e. they have no element in common
3. a finite set of re-write rules R of the form $A \longrightarrow BC$ or $A \longrightarrow a$ with $A, B, C \in V_n$ and $a \in V_t$
4. a start symbol $S \in V_n$ which is called the axiom of the grammar.

A grammar of this type 'generates' the sentences of a language by replacing a certain symbol such as A by a sequence of symbols, which are in turn replaced by other sequences of symbols until the final string (the sentence) is reached. The possibilities for replacing symbols are defined by the rules of the grammar and these must be formulated so as to generate the sentences of one particular language only. As set out above, a definition of a context-free grammar requires specification of the symbols that may occur and the rules for replacing those symbols.

Since the process of development is being traced in this study as changes in the likelihood of application of the rules, a method for weighting the rules of the grammar must also be defined. The system of weighting applied in the following was developed by Salomaa (1969). This is described in the section following the presentation of the grammar.

3.2 Description of the Grammar

The syntactic categories listed below such as VEGR - verbal group, NOGR - nominal group etc. constitute the auxiliary vocabulary (V_n) of the grammar and do not correspond to the traditional word classes such as 'noun' and 'verb' but are defined by their status in the system of rules. NOGR, the nominal group, includes not only single nouns but groupings consisting of adjectives + noun, adverbs and adjective + noun. The function of each rule of grammar will be described in detail below.

The grammar was adapted to the scope of the present study: it contains no terminal vocabulary, i.e. there are no rules of the form $A \longrightarrow a$, and morphological features of the learner language were also excluded. In this grammar PROP is defined as the axiom instead of S.

The rules are grouped into six syntactic complexes, the first group P1-P7 relates to the sentence level, the verbal complex (VEGR) is generated by rules V1-V29, subordinate clauses by rules S1-S9 (NESA), nominal groups (NOGR) by rules N1-N8, adverbials and adjectives rules A1-A12 and relative clauses by R1 and R2.

3.3 List of Rules with their Labels

P1	PROP	→ PRON	VEGR	(p.21)*
P2	PROP	→ ADVE	VEGR	(p.22)
P3	PROP	→ ADVE	PROP	(p.22)
P4	PROP	→ PROP	ADVE	(p.22)
P5	PROP	→ PROP	NOGR	(p.23)
P7	PROP	→ NOGR	VEGR	(p.23)
V1	VEGR	→ VEGR	NOGR	(p.24)
V2	VEGR	→ VEGR	ADVE	(p.26)
V3	VEGR	→ VEGR	ADJE	(p.27)
V4	VEGR	→ AUXI	VEGR	(p.32)
V5	VEGR	→ VEGR	PROP	(p.27)
V6	VEGR	→ VEGR	PRON	(p.28)
V7	VEGR	→ VEGR	REFW	(p.28)
V8	VEGR	→ VEGR	AFFI	(p.28)
V9	VEGR	→ PRON	VEGR	(p.37)
V10	VEGR	→ ADVE	VEGR	(p.37)
V11	VEGR	→ VEGR	AUXI	(p.39)
V12	VEGR	→ ADJE	VEGR	(p.38)
V13	VEGR	→ NOGR	VEGR	(p.38)
V14	VEGR	→ ADJE	VEGR	(p.34)
V15	VEGR	→ VEGR	PRON	(p.31)
V16	VEGR	→ ZUWO	VEGR	(p.34)
V17	VEGR	→ PRON	VEGR	(p.33)
V18	VEGR	→ ADVE	VEGR	(p.35)
V19	VEGR	→ VEGR	NESA	(p.29)
V20	VEGR	→ VEGR	INFR	(p.30)
V21	VEGR	→ VEGR	NESA	(p.30)
V22	VEGR	→ NOGR	VEGR	(p.33)
V23	VEGR	→ VEGR	NESA	(p.31)

S1	NESA	→ KONJ	VEGR	(35)
S2	NESA	→ KONJ	PROP	(39)
S3	NESA	→ ADVE	VEGR	(41)
S4	NESA	→ NOGR	VEGR	(40)
S5	NESA	→ KONJ	VEGR	(36)
S6	NESA	→ KONJ	PROP	(39)
S7	NESA	→ KONJ	VEGR	(36)
S8	NESA	→ KONJ	PROP	(40)
S9	NESA	→ KONJ	VEGR	(36)
R1	RELS	→ RELW	VEGR	(40)
R2	INFR	→ FRWO	VEGR	(41)
A1	ADVE	→ PRÄP	NOGR	(42)
A3	ADJE	→ ADJE	NOGR	(42)
A4	ADJE	→ ADVE	ADJE	(42)
A5	ADVE	→ ADJE	NOGR	(42)
A7	ADVE	→ KONJ	ADVE	(42)
A9	ADVE	→ ADVE	ADVE	(42)
A10	ADVE	→ ADVE	NESA	(42)
A12	ADJE	→ ADJE	NESA	(42)
N1	NOGR	→ PRÄP	NOGR	(42)
N2	NOGR	→ ADJE	NOGR	(42)
N3	NOGR	→ NOGR	NOGR	(42)
N4	NOGR	→ KONJ	NOGR	(42)
N5	NOGR	→ NOGR	RELS	(42)
N6	NOGR	→ ADVE	NOGR	(42)
N7	NOGR	→ NOGR	ADJE	(42)
N8	NOGR	→ NOGR	ADVE	(42)

*This refers to the page on which the rules are defined.

V25 VEGR → NOGR VEGR (p.38)
V26 VEGR → PRON VEGR (p.39)
V27 VEGR → VEGR NOGR (p.32)
V28 VEGR → PRON VEGR (p.33)
V29 VEGR → NOGR VEGR (p.33)

3.4 Notation of the Syntactic Categories

These rules as presented below are written in "complex notation".[6] The general idea behind this system of notation is as follows: The syntactic category is represented as consisting of a main category and a sub-category which encompasses various features. The main category is represented by four higher-case letters, NOGR, for instance, the features by three lower-case letters such as 'gen' for gender, or 'num' for number etc. Every feature such as 'gen' is a function with a finite set of two or more integers as arguments which describe the values the feature can take. The feature 'gen' (i.e. gender), for instance, can take three values:

gen (1) = masculine (mas)
gen (2) = feminine (fem)
gen (3) = neuter (neu)

where the number in brackets is the argument and mas, fem, neu are the values of the function 'gen'. Furthermore, in this system of notation, gen (3) is a specified feature; 'gen' on its own is an unspecified feature.

In this system of notation a syntactic category is represented by the subcategory:

NOGR
num (2)
gen (1)
cas (4)

This example, for instance, symbolises all dative, plural, masculine nouns where num (1) = singular, num (2) = plural number, gen (1) = masculine, gen (2) = feminine, gen (3) = neuter gender, cas (1) = nominative, cas (2) = accusative, cas (3) = genitive and cas (4) = dative case.

---

[6]This system of notation was developed by Brockhaus (1971) and is described in detail in Kratzer et al.(1974).

This specification of syntactic categories in terms of a main and sub-category permits the grouping of rules which are related to each other, as shown in the following example:

```
NOGR  num (1) gen (2) cas (2) ——>  KONJ  NOGR num (1) gen (2) cas (2)
NOGR  num (2) gen (1) cas (1) ——>  KONJ  NOGR num (2) gen (1) cas (1)
NOGR  num (1) gen (3) cas (4) ——>  KONJ  NOGR num (1) gen (3) cas (4)
```

These are three "elementary" rules which can be grouped to form a complex rule as follows:

NOGR ——————————>	KONJ	NOGR	sub-category congruence
num		num	(1, 0, 1)
gen		gen	(2, 0, 2)
cas		cas	(3, 0, 3)

In the elementary rules above the arguments of num, gen, cas following the leftmost symbol NOGR correspond to the arguments of the features appearing under NOGR on the right of the arrow (i.e. after replacement of the symbol NOGR with KONJ NOGR).[7] These conditions are now summarised in the column "sub-category congruence". The three places in the brackets apply, reading from left to right, to the three main categories which form the rule. The number in the first place always applies to the first main category, the one in the second to the second category, and so on. On the other hand if their value is 1, it refers to the <u>first feature</u> listed under the main category in question, 2 refers to the <u>second feature</u> in the first, i.e. gen, 3 to cas etc. In other words, 2 in the third place of the bracket refers to the second feature listed under the third main category given in the rule, i.e. NOGR; 0, which occupies the second place reading from left to right, applies to KONJ, the value is 0 since there are no features listed.
The grouping of elementary rules in this way is subject to the following set of conventions:

1. An unspecified feature occurring only once in a rule can take any of its possible values.

---

[7] If the noun in question was masculine, for instance, before being replaced it must remain so afterwards.

2. An unspecified feature occurring twice or three times in a rule must be specified with the same argument (which can be any of the alternatives) in all cases.

3. If a feature occurring twice or three times in a rule has been specified only once, this specification applies for the others.

4. Different features can be specified independently.

5. Specifications should not be contradictory.

3.5 List of Main Categories and Their Features.

Main Category		Features
PROP	...	sub, aux
VEGR	...	sub, ord, aty, cty, dty, ety, fty, rty, omz, aux
NESA	...	dty
AUXI	...	-
NOGR	...	-
ADVE	...	-
ADJE	...	-
RELS	...	-
KONJ	...	-
ZUWO	...	-
REFW	...	-
RELW	...	-
FRWO	...	-
AFFI	...	-

Explanation of the Features

Features	Argument	Meaning
sub (at VEGR)	(1)	Saturated with respect to PRON/NOGR
	(2)	VEGR not preceded by PRON/NOGR
	(3)	VEGR adds on PRON/NOGR or RELW (relative pronouns)
	(4)	Participle
	(5)	Infinitive

sub (at PROP)	(1)	String with PRON/NOGR in initial position
	(2)	String with ADVE in initial position
ord	(1)	Verb in second position in clause
	(2)	Subordinate clause order of elements (i.e. verb at end of clause)
aty	(0)	Saturated with respect to NOGR
	(1)	Adds on NOGR
cty	(0)	Saturated with respect to AFFIX
	(1)	Adds on AFFIX
dty at VEGR)	(0)	Saturated with respect to 'daß-clause' infinitives, indirect- question clauses, PROP
	(1)	Adds on daß-clause
	(2)	Adds on infinitive
	(3)	Adds on indirect-question clause (INFR)
	(4)	Adds on PROP
dty (at NESA)	(1)	Daß-clause (<u>that</u> clause)
	(4)	Wenn-clause (<u>when</u>/<u>if</u>)
	(5)	Weil-clause (<u>because</u>)
	(6)	Wie-clause (<u>how</u>)
	(2)	Infinitive
ety	(0)	Saturated with respect to ADVE
	(1)	Adds on ADVE
fty	(0)	Saturated with respect to ADJE
	(1)	Adds on ADJE
rty	(0)	Saturated with respect to REFW (i.e. reflexive forms)
	(1)	Adds on REFW
omz	(0)	Saturated with respect to ZUWO
	(1)	Adds on ZUWO (i.e. infinitive "to")
aux	(0)	VEGR with no auxiliary
	(1)	VEGR with auxiliary, no NOGR in subject position
	(2)	VEGR with auxiliary, NOGR in subject position
(at all categories)	(+)	None of the defined values

These features and their values form the sub-categories of the main categories. (+) can occur in all sub-categories and means that the main category need not be specified with respect to the sub-category in question.

3.6 The PROP-Rules

P1 specifies that PROP can be re-written as PRON VEGR. The PROP rules also show which category appears in the initial position in the final string, i.e. in the sentence; with P1 this is PRON, a pronoun. If rule P2 or P3 is applied the first category is ADVE, an adverbial phrase, with P7 the first category is NOGR, a noun phrase.

P1

PROP	→	PRON	VEGR	Sub-categ. congruence
sub (1)			sub (3)	
aux			ord (1)	
			aty (0)	
			cty (0,+)	
			dty (0)	
			ety (0)	
			fty (0)	
			rty (0,+)	
			omz (0,+)	
			aux (0,1)	(2,0,10)

cf. Example 1. p. 109

P1 states that a PROP of type sub (1) is formed by taking a PRON and a VEGR of type sub (3). The feature sub specifies that this VEGR takes a NOGR/PRON complement (subject noun phrase). This corresponds to the definition of sub, in this case (1), at PROP (cf. feature meanings p. 20). The second feature listed under PROP, i.e. aux, specifies that PROP may or may not have an auxiliary verb. Correspondence is required between the value of aux at PROP and that of aux at VEGR. This requirement is expressed by sub-category congruence conditions (2,0,10) which reads as follows: 2 corresponds to the second feature listed under PROP i.e. aux, 0 refers to the next category PRON and specifies that no congruence requirements apply, 10 corresponds to the 10th feature listed under VEGR, i.e. aux, if aux is (1) under PROP it must also be (1) under VEGR. In other words, the conditions always read from left to right in accordance with the sequence of categories in the rule, the figure refers to the position in the list of features. Congruence at aux is required in order to restrict application of rules P4 and P5 to strings generating auxiliary verbs. Structures described by P4 and P5 occur after strings with auxiliary verbs only. The specification aux (0) is excluded here.

P2

PROP	→	ADVE	VEGR	Sub-categ. congruence
sub (2)			sub (2)	(1,0,1)
aux			ord (1)	
			aty (0)	
			cty (0,+)	
			dty (0)	
			ety (0)	
			fty (0)	
			rty (0,+)	
			omz (0,+)	
			aux (0,1)	(2,0,10)

cf. Example 2. p. 110

P2 states that a PROP of type sub (2) is formed by taking an ADVE and a VEGR of type sub (2). ADVE appears in the initial position in the final string and VEGR type sub (2) specifies that this VEGR is followed by PRON/NOGR. This rule describes structures in which S + V sequences are inverted after ADVE in the initial position.

P3

PROP	→	ADVE	PROP	Sub-categ. congruence
sub (2)			sub (1)	
aux			aux	(2,0,2)

cf. Example 6. p. 115

P3 states that a PROP of type sub (2) is formed by taking an ADVE and a PROP of type sub (1). This rule describes structures with an adverbial phrase in the initial position in the string not followed by inversion of the subject verb sequence.

P4

PROP	→	PROP	ADVE	Sub-categ. congruence
sub		sub (1,2)		(1,1,0)
aux		aux (1,2)		(2,2,0)

cf. Example 5. p.114

P4 states that a PROP of type sub (1,2) is formed by taking a PROP of the same type and an ADVE. aux (1,2) specifies that this string must contain an auxiliary verb. This rule generates structures where ADVE appears outside the sentence frame as in "Ich habe gestern gesessen, hier". As with P5 (see below) there is no limit on the number of ADVE or NOGR which can be generated by these rules.

P5

PROP	⟶ PROP	NOGR	Sub-categ. congruence
sub	sub (1,2)		(1,1,0)
aux	aux (1,2)		(2,2,0)

cf. Example 3. p. 111

P5 is similar to P4 except that here NOGR appears outside the sentence frame.

P7

PROP	⟶ NOGR	VEGR	Sub-categ. congruence
sub (1)		sub (3)	
aux		ord (1)	
		aty (0)	
		cty (0,+)	
		dty (0)	
		ety (0)	
		fty (0)	
		rty (0,+)	
		omz (+)	
		aux (0,2)	(2,0,10)

cf. Example 1, p. 109

P7 is similar to P1 except that here NOGR, a noun phrase, appears in the initial position in the string. The function of the specification <u>aux</u> (0,2) is explained under rules V28/29 p.33.

3.7 The VEGR-Rules V1-V29

The rules V1, V2, V3, V5, V7, V8, V15, V27 and V19-23 generate structures in which elements of the final string appear to the right of VEGR. This applies to constituents in predicative position occurring in strings with the following order of elements: S + V + X and ADVE + V + S + X. Subordinate clauses, where verbs appear in the final position, are not generated by these 'right-adjoining' rules.

The rules V4, V14, V16, V17, V18, V22 V28 and V29 generate strings with auxiliary verbs and participles. Participles are described by the main category VEGR but are specified by the feature sub (4).
The rules V9, V25, V10, V11, V12, V13 and V26 generate final strings in which VEGR appears in the final position. These 'left-adjoining' rules describe subordinate clauses with conjunctions in the initial position which are generated by the rules S1, S5, S7, S9 and were analysed separately.

'Right-adjoining' VEGR Rules

Although we have no certifiable intuitions as to what is acceptable in learner languages this grammar generates, in addition to the regularities observed, strings which would hardly be acceptable and, secondly, would not be producible. This applies, in particular, to the recursivity of the rules V1, V2, V3, as well as to P4, P5 above. No restrictions have been set on the number of complements of a particular type a verb can take, nor have the complements been specified as to the verb types which they conjoin, as would be required in a more complete definition of this grammar.

V1

VEGR ⟶	VEGR	NOGR	Sub-categ.congruence
sub	sub (2,3)		(1,1,0)
ord	ord (1)		(2,2,0)
aty (0,1)	aty (1)		
cty	cty		(4,4,0)
dty	dty		(5,5,0)
ety	ety		(6,6,0)
fty	fty (0)		(7,7,0)
rty	rty (0)		(8,8,0)
omz	omz (+)		(9,9,0)
aux	aux (0)		(10,10,0)

cf. Example 1, p. 109.

This rule states that a VEGR of type aty (0,1) is formed by taking a VEGR of type aty (1) and a NOGR (aty (1) specifies that VEGR requires a noun complement). aty (0) states that the VEGR is saturated with respect to this complement. The specification aty (0,1) permits recursive application of this rule where necessary. In a 'bottom up' analysis, for instance, where two NOGRs are present in the sentence, aty is specified as (1) until both complements have been adjoined. The number of NOGR which can be adjoined to a VEGR of this type is therefore unrestricted, a verb of this type can take any number of noun complements.

The values of the remaining features define which rules can be applied in conjunction with V1. Applicability is first of all restricted to 'right-adjoining' rules only, marked by ord (1). In other words, for a rule to be applicable, the values of the features in the respective rule must coincide with those defined in V1.

sub (2,3) specifies that this is a VEGR where the first noun phrase (subject of the sentence) is adjoined to the VEGR, as defined by sub (3), or where the first noun phrase is adjoined to the right of VEGR, as defined by sub (2). sub (3) applies in strings where the sequence of elements is similar to that of declarative sentences, sub (2) in strings with inversion of the S + V sequence to V + S. In the latter context right-adjoinment of the first noun phrase (subject) requires application of V15 (not V1). sub, therefore, specifies adjoinment of subject noun phrases.

cty, dty, ety and fty which regulate the adjoinment of various verb complements (see feature meanings p. 20) are not specified here since all of their possible values can apply in conjunction with V1.

cty refers to application of the rule V8 whereby an AFFIX is adjoined to the VEGR. Specification is not restricted, i.e. it can be (0) or (1). In order to prevent generation of strings in which a noun complement (NOGR) appears after AFFIX in the final string (Ich bring mit das Buch), V8 can only be applied when aty is (0), i.e. when NOGR has been adjoined or is not required. The definition of restrictions is based on observations of regularities in the data, with the exception of V1, V2 and V3 where the number of complements which can be added to VEGR is unrestricted, although no such structures were observed in the data. The maximum number occurring together is two.

dty refers to the application of rules V23 - dty (1) (that clause), V19 - dty (2), V21 - dty (2) infinitives, V5 - dty (4) (VEGR takes PROP, i.e. a main clause as complement). V23 can be applied in conjunction with V1 only when aty is (0) (see aty at V23). This prevents the generation of strings in which a 'that clause' appears in the sentence before a noun phrase complement.

ety refers to application of rule V2. All values defined for ety can apply.

fty refers to rule V3 and is specified here with (0) as is aty at V3. This excludes application of V1 in conjunction with V3. VEGR cannot take a noun phrase as well as an adjectival phrase complement at the same time.

rty refers to application of rule V7. rty is (0) here and is specified in this sub-group of 'right-adjoining' VEGR-rules with (0) in order to ensure that reflexive words (sich helfen, help oneself) are adjoined to VEGR before all other complements, with the exception of sub.

omz (+) means none of the values of the feature omz applies here.

aux specifies VEGRs with an auxiliary verb (i.e. both modal and auxiliary forms).

The congruence requirements specify that the values of the respective sub-categories must be identical. If sub is (2) on the left-hand side, for instance, it must be re-written as (2) (and not 3), or vice versa.

V2

VEGR	⟶ VEGR	ADVE	Sub-categ. congruence
sub	sub (2,3)		(1,1,0)
ord	ord (1)		(2,2,0)
aty	aty		(3,3,0)
cty	cty		(4,4,0)
dty	dty		(5,5,0)
ety (0,1)	ety (1)		
fty	fty		(7,7,0)
rty	rty (0)		(8,8,0)
omz	omz (+)		(9,9,0)
aux	aux (0)		(10,10,0)

cf. Example 2. p.110

This rule states that a VEGR of type ety (0,1) is formed by taking a VEGR of type ety (1) and an ADVE. The repeated specification of ety (1) in ety (0,1) permits recursive application of this rule. All values of the features aty, cty, dty and fty can apply in conjunction with V2. Congruence is required between the selected values however.

rty, omz and aux are defined as in rule V1.

V3

VEGR ⟶	VEGR	ADJE	Sub-categ. congruence
sub	sub (2,3)		(1,1,0)
ord	ord (1)		)2,2,0)
aty	aty (0)		(3,3,0)
cty	cty		(4,4,0)
dty	dty (0)		
ety	ety		(6,6,0)
fty (0,1)	fty (1)		
rty	rty (0)		(8,8,0)
omz	omz (+)		(9,9,0)
aux	aux (0)		(10,10,0)

cf. Example 4. p. 112

This rule states that a VEGR of type fty (0,1) is formed by taking a VEGR of type fty (1) and ADJE. <u>dty</u> is specified (0). All remaining features are defined as in V1.

V5

VEGR ⟶	VEGR	PROP	Sub-categ. congruence
sub	sub (2,3)	sub (1,2)	(1,1,0)
ord	ord (1)	aux	(2,2,0)
aty	aty (0)		(3,3,0)
cty	cty (0)		(4,4,0)
dty (0)	dty (4)		
ety	ety (0)		(6,6,0)
fty	fty (0)		(7,7,0)
rty	rty (0)		(8,8,0)
omz	omz (+)		(9,9,0)
aux	aux		(10,10,0)

cf. Example 9. p. 118

A VEGR of type dty (0) is formed by taking a VEGR of type dty (4) and a PROP. Specification of the other features with (0) means that V5 can be applied only when these are saturated (or are not required). <u>aux</u> is not restricted to a specific value as in the preceding rules, i.e. strings generated by V5 may contain auxiliary verbs.

V6

VEGR	→ VEGR	PRON	Sub-categ. congruence
sub	sub (2,3)		(1,1,0)
ord	ord (1)		(2,2,0)
aty (0,1)	aty (1)		
cty	cty		(4,4,0)
dty	dty		(5,5,0)
ety	ety		(6,6,0)
fty	fty (0)		(7,7,0)
rty	rty (0)		(8,8,0)
omz	omz (+)		(9,9,0)
aux	aux (0)		(10,10,0)

cf. Example 1. p. 109

V6 is similar to V1, except that here PRON is adjoined to VEGR instead of NOGR.

V7

VEGR	→ VEGR	REFW	Sub-categ. congruence
sub	sub (2,3)		(1,1,0)
ord	ord (1)		(2,2,0)
aty	aty		(3,3,0)
cty	cty		(4,4,0)
dty	dty		(5,5,0)
ety	ety		(6,6,0)
fty	fty		(7,7,0)
rty (0)	rty (1)		
omz	omz (+)		(9,9,0)
aux	aux (0)		(10,10,0)

cf. Example 9. p. 118

This rule states that a VEGR of type rty (0) is formed by taking a VEGR of type rty (1) and REFW. The values of the remaining complements are not restricted to any one of the possible values. Congruence requirements hold as defined.

V8

VEGR	→ VEGR	AFFI	Sub-categ. congruence
sub	sub (2,3)		(1,1,0)
ord	ord (1)		(2,2,0)
aty	aty (0)		(3,3,0)
cty (0)	cty (1)		
dty	dty		(5,5,0)
ety	ety (0)		(6,6,0)
fty	fty (0)		(7,7,0)
rty	rty (0)		(8,8,0)
omz	omz (+)		(9,9,0)
aux	aux (0)		(10,10,0)

cf. Example 10. p. 119

A VEGR of type <u>cty</u> (0) is formed by taking a VEGR of type <u>cty</u> (1) and AFFI. In order to ensure that AFFI occurs in end-position in the final string, V8 can be applied only when all other complements are saturated (0), or are not required.

<u>omz</u> and <u>aux</u> are specified as in rule V6 and V7.

V19

VEGR →	VEGR	NESA	Sub-categ. congruence
sub	sub (3)	dty (2)	(1,1,0)
ord	ord (1)		(2,2,0)
aty	aty (0)		(3,3,0)
cty	cty (0,+)		(4,4,0)
dty (0)	dty (2)		(0,5,1)
ety	ety (0)		(6,6,0)
fty	fty (0)		(7,7,0)
rty	rty (0,+)		(8,8,0)
omz	omz (+)		(9,9,0)
aux	aux		(10,10,0)

cf. Example 8. p. 117

This rule states that a VEGR of type <u>dty</u> (0) is formed by taking a VEGR of type <u>dty</u> (2) and NESA. V19 describes what is actually a noun phrase complement as the following example shows:

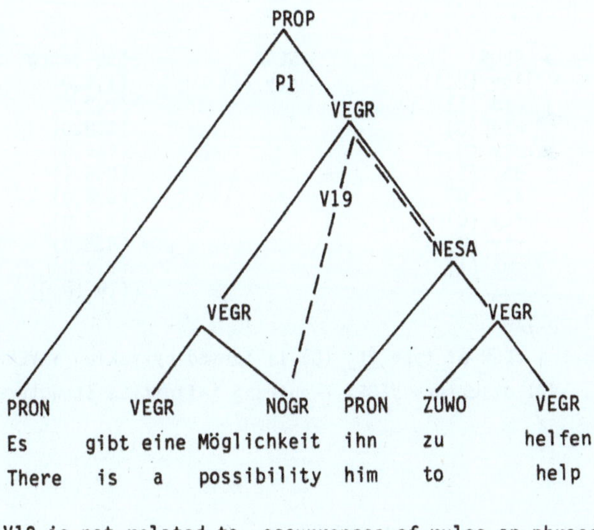

In this way V19 is not related to occurrences of rules on phrase level but to possible expansions on sentence level, i.e. to PROP rules. This ad-hoc solution was adopted here since the method of analysis measures probabilities of transition between two elements only. Correct measurement can be made by using probabilities of occurrence of larger sequences of rules - given a + b, what is the probability that c will occur, for instance? The occurrence of c would be thereby linked to a.

V20

VEGR	→ VEGR	INFR	Sub-categ. congruence
sub	sub (2,3)		(1,1,0)
ord	ord (1)		(2,2,0)
aty	aty (0)		(3,3,0)
cty	cty (0,+)		(4,4,0)
dty (0)	dty (3)		
ety	ety (0)		(6,6,0)
fty	fty (0)		(7,7,0)
rty	rty (0,+)		(8,8,0)
omz	omz (+)		(9,9,0)
aux	aux		(10,10,0)

cf. Example 12. p. 121

V20 states that a VEGR of type <u>dty</u> (0) is formed by taking a VEGR of type <u>dty</u> (3) and INFR. <u>dty</u> (3) refers to VEGRs requiring w- clauses as compleme-nts. W clauses refer to <u>how</u>, <u>where</u>, <u>what</u>, i.e. <u>wie</u>, <u>wo</u>, <u>was</u> etc.

V21

VEGR	→ VEGR	NESA	Sub-categ. congruence
sub	sub (2,3)	dty (2)	(1,1,0)
ord	ord (1)		(2,2,0)
aty	aty (0)		(3,3,0)
cty	cty (0,+)		(4,4,0)
dty (0)	dty (2)		(0,5,1)
ety	ety (0)		(6,6,0)
fty	fty (0)		(7,7,0)
rty	rty (0,+)		(8,8,0)
omz	omz (+)		(9,9,0)
aux	aux		(10,10,0)

cf. Example 7. p.116

V21 states that a VEGR of type <u>dty</u> (0) is formed by taking a VEGR of type <u>dty</u> (2) and NESA. V21 describes VEGRs requiring infinitive structures as comple-ments.

V23

VEGR		VEGR	NESA	Sub-categ. congruence
sub	→	sub (3)	dty (1)	(1,1,0)
ord		ord (1,2)		(2,2,0)
aty		aty (0)		(3,3,0)
cty		cty (0,+)		(4,4,0)
dty (0)		dty (1)		(0,5,1)
ety		ety (0)		(6,6,0)
fty		fty (0)		(7,7,0)
rty		rty (0,+)		(8,8,0)
omz		omz (+)		(9,9,0)
aux		aux		(10,10,0)

cf. Example 12. p. 121

This rule states that a VEGR of type <u>dty</u> (0) is formed by taking a VEGR of type <u>dty</u> (1) and NESA. This rule describes VEGRs requiring that-clauses as complements.

Rules V19-V23 differ from V1, V2, V3, V5, V6, V7 and V8 in respect of their sub-categories: the features <u>cty</u> and <u>rty</u> are specified as (0,+) which permits application of the former group of rules in conjunction with those generating structures with auxiliary verbs (see example 7. p.116). Congruence is required between <u>dty</u> at VEGR and <u>dty</u> at NESA.

V15

VEGR		VEGR	PRON	Sub-categ. congruence
sub (2)	→	sub (3)		
ord		ord (1)		(2,2,0)
aty		aty		(3,3,0)
cty		cty		(4,4,0)
dty		dty		(5,5,0)
ety		ety		(6,6,0)
fty		fty		(7,7,0)
rty		rty		(8,8,0)
omz		omz (+)		(9,9,0)
aux		aux (0)		(10,10,0)

cf. Example 2. p.110

V15 states that a VEGR of type <u>sub</u> (2) is formed by taking a VEGR of type <u>sub</u> (3) and a PRON. This rule is applied in strings with inversion of the subject verb sequence and specifies that this VEGR adjoins PRON (subject) on its right.

V27

VEGR	→	VEGR	NOGR	Sub-categ. congruence
sub (2)		sub (3)		
ord		ord (1)		(2,2,0)
aty		aty		(3,3,0)
cty		cty		(4,4,0)
dty		dty		(5,5,0)
ety		ety		(6,6,0)
fty		fty		(7,7,0)
rty		rty		(8,8,0)
omz		omz (+)		(9,9,0)
aux		aux (0)		(10,10,0)

cf. Example 2. p. 110

V27 is similar to V15 except that here NOGR is adjoined to VEGR.

Rules V4, V14, V16, V17, V18, V22, V28 and V29 generate strings with auxiliary verbs. In this group of rules complements are adjoined to the left of VEGR (here participle or infinitive) and are therefore specified as *ord* (2). *sub* (4) describes participles, *sub* (5) infinitives.

V4

VEGR	→	AUXI	VEGR	Sub-categ. congruence
sub (2,3)			sub (4,5)	
ord (1)			ord (2)	
aty			aty (0)	(3,0,3)
cty			cty (+)	(4,0,4)
dty			dty	(5,0,5)
ety			ety (0)	(6,0,6)
fty			fty (0)	(7,0,7)
rty			rty (+)	(8,0,8)
omz			omz (+)	(9,0,9)
aux			aux (1,2)	(10,0,10)

cf. Example 8. p. 117

V4 states that a VEGR of type *sub* (2,3), *ord* (1) is formed by taking a VEGR of type *sub* (4,5), *ord* (2) and AUXI.

cty (+) and *rty* (+) means that none of the specified values apply here. VEGRs in this sub-order do not take complements of this type.

aux (1,2) specifies that this VEGR has an auxiliary verb. *aux* (2) ensures restriction of the application of rules V28 and V29 (cf. comment on these rules).

V17 / V22

VEGR	→ PRON	VEGR	Sub-categ. congruence
VEGR	→ NOGR	VEGR	
sub		sub (4,5)	(1,0,1)
ord		ord (2)	(2,0,2)
aty (0,1)		aty (1)	
cty		cty (+)	(4,0,4)
dty		dty	(5,0,5)
ety		ety	(6,0,6)
fty		fty (0)	(7,0,7)
rty		rty (+)	(8,0,8)
omz		omz (+)	(9,0,9)
aux		aux (1)	(10,0,10)

cf. Example 3. p.111

V17 and V22 state that a VEGR of type aty (0,1) is formed by taking a VEGR of aty (1) and PRON/NOGR. The subject noun phrase is also adjoined to VEGR by means of these rules in strings with auxiliary verbs and inversion of the subject verb sequence, as in "dann hat er uns das Buch gegeben", "then has he us the book given".

aux (1) excludes adjoinment of V28/V29 (see below).

V28 / V29

VEGR	→ PRON	VEGR	Sub-categ. congruence
VEGR	→ NOGR	VEGR	
sub		sub (4,5)	(1,0,1)
ord		ord (2)	(2,0,2)
aty (0,1)		aty (1)	
cty		cty (+)	(4,0,4)
dty		dty	(5,0,5)
ety		ety	(6,0,6)
fty		fty (0)	(7,0,7)
rty		rty (+)	(8,0,8)
omz		omz (0)	(9,0,9)
aux		aux (2)	(10,0,10)

cf. Example 3. p. 111

These rules differ from V17 and V22 only in respect of the feature aux which is specified here as (2). The application of these rules is restricted to cases where the subject consists of a noun phrase and not a pronoun. V28 and V29 are applied in conjunction with P7 only. These rules have the function of marking the presence of NOGR in subject position. In all tree diagrams of sentences with auxiliary verbs V4 occurs between Pl or P7 and rules generating structures which appear in predicative position. In example 5, for instance, p.114, the control word of the diagram reads P4 Al Pl V4 V18. The transitions measured here are P4 Al, Al Pl, Pl V4, V4 V18. Therefore, no connection can be made between the occurrence of Pl and V18. As with V19 above, such relationships should be documented by weighting probabilities of larger sequences of rules.

V14

VEGR → ADJE	VEGR	Sub-categ. congruence
sub	sub (4,5)	(1,0,1)
ord	ord (2)	(2,0,2)
aty	aty	(3,0,3)
cty	cty (+)	(4,0,4)
dty	dty (0)	(5,0,5)
ety	ety	(6,0,6)
fty (0,1)	fty (1)	
rty	rty (+)	(8,0,8)
omz	omz (+)	(9,0,9)
aux	aux (1,2)	(10,0,10)

cf. Example 11. p. 120

V14 states that a VEGR of type <u>fty</u> (0,1) is formed by taking a VEGR of type <u>fty</u> (1) and ADJE.

V16

VEGR → ZUWO	VEGR	Sub-categ. congruence
sub	sub (5)	(1,0,1)
ord	ord (2)	(2,0,2)
aty	aty	(3,0,3)
cty	cty (0)	(4,0,4)
dty	dty	(5,0,5)
ety	ety	(6,0,6)
fty	fty	(7,0,7)
rty	rty (0)	(8,0,8)
omz (0)	omz (1)	
aux	aux	(10,0,10)

cf. Example 8. p. 117

V16 states that a VEGR of type <u>omz</u> (0) is formed by taking a VEGR of type <u>omz</u> (1) and ZUWO. <u>omz</u> (1) describes infinitives requiring 'to'.

V18

VEGR ⟶ ADVE	VEGR	Sub-categ. congruence
sub	sub (4,5)	(1,0,1)
ord	ord (2)	(2,0,2)
aty	aty	(3,0,3)
cty	cty (+)	(4,0,4)
dty	dty	(5,0,5)
ety (0,1)	ety (1)	
fty	fty	(7,0,7)
rty	rty (+)	(8,0,8)
omz	omz (+)	(9,0,9)
aux	aux (1,2)	(10,0,10)

cf. Example 5. p. 114

V18 states that a VEGR of type _ety_ (0,1) is formed by taking a VEGR of type _ety_ (1) and ADVE.

3.8 Subordinate Clause Rules

The rules S1, S5, S7 and S9 generate strings with KONJ in the initial position, while VEGR occupies the final position in the clauses as required in German.

S1

NESA ⟶	KONJ	VEGR
dty (1)		sub (1)
		ord (2)
		aty (0)
		cty (+)
		dty (+)
		ety (0)
		fty (0)
		rty (+)
		omz (+)
		aux

cf. Example 14. p. 123

S5

NESA dty (4)	⟶ KONJ	VEGR sub (1) ord (2) aty (0) cty (+) dty (+) ety (0) fty (0) rty (+) omz (+) aux

cf. Example 4a. p. 113

S7

NESA dty (5)	⟶ KONJ	VEGR sub (1) ord (2) aty (0) cty (+) dty (+) ety (0) fty (0) rty (+) omz (+) aux

cf. Example 13. p. 122

S9

NESA dty (6)	⟶ KONJ	VEGR sub (1) ord (2) aty (0) cty (+) dty (+) ety (0) fty (0) rty (+) omz (+) aux

All four are identical and differ only in respect of the type of conjunction adjoined. dty (1) Daß; dty (4) Wenn; dty (5) Weil; dty (6) Wie.

The rules V9 - V13 generate strings in which the constituents of the final string appear to the left of VEGR (subordinate clauses).

V9

VEGR ⟶	PRON	VEGR	Sub-categ. congruence
sub (1)		sub (3)	
ord		ord (2)	(2,0,2)
aty		aty (0)	(3,0,3)
cty		cty (+)	(4,0,4)
dty		dty (+)	(5,0,5)
ety		ety (0)	(6,0,6)
fty		fty (0)	(7,0,7)
rty		rty (+)	(8,0,8)
omz		omz (+)	(9,0,9)
aux		aux	(10,0,10)

cf. Example 4a. p. 113

This rule states that a VEGR of type <u>sub</u> (1) is formed by taking a VEGR of type <u>sub</u> (3) and PRON.

V10

VEGR ⟶	ADVE	VEGR	Sub-categ. congruence
sub		sub (3)	(1,0,1)
ord		ord (2)	(2,0,2)
aty		aty	(3,0,3)
cty		cty (+)	(4,0,4)
dty		dty (+)	(5,0,5)
ety (0)		ety (1)	
fty		fty	(7,0,7)
rty		rty (+)	(8,0,8)
omz		omz (+)	(9,0,9)
aux		aux	(10,0,10)

cf. Example 13. p. 122

This rule states that a VEGR of type <u>ety</u> (0) is formed by taking a VEGR of type <u>ety</u> (1) and ADVE.

V12

VEGR ⟶ ADJE	VEGR	Sub-categ. congruence
sub (3)	sub (3,4)	
ord	ord (2)	(2,0,2)
aty	aty	(3,0,3)
cty	cty (+)	(4,0,4)
dty	dty (+)	(5,0,5)
ety	ety	(6,0,6)
fty (0)	fty (1)	
rty	rty (+)	(8,0,8)
omz	omz (+)	(9,0,9)
aux	aux	(10,0,10)

cf. Example 13. p. 122

This rule states that a VEGR of type <u>fty</u> (0) is formed by taking a VEGR of type <u>fty</u> (1) and ADJE.

V13

VEGR ⟶ NOGR	VEGR	Sub-categ. congruence
sub	sub (3)	(1,0,1)
ord	ord (2)	(2,0,2)
aty (0,1)	aty (1)	
cty	cty (+)	(4,0,4)
dty	dty (+)	(5,0,5)
ety	ety	(6,0,6)
fty	fty (0)	(7,0,7)
rty	rty (+)	(8,0,8)
omz	omz (+)	(9,0,9)
aux	aux	(10,0,10)

cf. Example 4a. p. 113

This rule states that a VEGR of type <u>aty</u> (0,1) is formed by taking a VEGR of type <u>aty</u> (1) and NOGR.

V25

VEGR ⟶ NOGR	VEGR	Sub-categ. congruence
sub (1)	sub (3)	
ord	ord (2)	(2,0,2)
aty	aty (0)	(3,0,3)
cty	cty (+)	(4,0,4)
dty	dty (+)	(5,0,5)
ety	ety (0)	(6,0,6)
fty	fty (0)	(7,0,7)
rty	rty (+)	(8,0,8)
omz	omz (+)	(9,0,9)
aux	aux	(10,0,10)

cf. Example 4a. p. 113

V25 is similar to V9 except that here NOGR is adjoined to VEGR.

V26

VEGR	⟶ PRON	VEGR	Sub-categ. congruence
sub		sub (3)	(1,0,1)
ord		ord (2)	(2,0,2)
aty (0)		aty (1)	
cty		cty (+)	(4,0,4)
dty		dty (+)	(5,0,5)
ety		ety	(6,0,6)
fty		fty (0)	(7,0,7)
rty		rty (+)	(8,0,8)
omz		omz (+)	(9,0,9)
aux		aux	(10,0,10)

cf. Example 4a. p. 113

V26 is similar to V13 except that here PRON is adjoined to VEGR.

V11

VEGR	⟶ VEGR	AUXI	Sub-categ. congruence
sub (3)	sub (4,5)		
ord	ord (2)		(2,0,2)
aty	aty		(3,0,3)
cty	cty (+)		(4,0,4)
dty	dty (+)		(5,0,5)
ety	ety		(6,0,6)
fty	fty		(7,0,7)
rty	rty (+)		(8,0,8)
omz	omz (+)		(9,0,9)
aux	aux (1)		(10,0,10)

cf. Example 13. p. 122

V11 states that a VEGR of type _sub_ (3) is formed by taking a VEGR of type _sub_ (4,5) and AUXI.

S2

NESA	⟶ KONJ	PROP
dty (1)		sub
		aux

cf. Example 12. p. 121

S6

NESA	⟶ KONJ	PROP
dty (4)		sub
		aux

S8

NESA	⟶	KONJ	PROP
dty (5)			sub
			aux

The rules S2, S6 and S8 generate subordinate clauses with conjunctions in the initial position while the verb occupies the third position in the clause (main clause word order).

S4

NESA	⟶	NOGR	VEGR
dty (2)			sub (5)
			ord (2)
			aty (1)
			cty (0)
			dty (0)
			ety (1)
			fty (0)
			rty (0)
			omz (0)
			aux

cf. Example 8. p. 117

S4 states that a NESA of type <u>dty</u> (2) is formed by taking a VEGR of type <u>sub</u> (5) (infinitive) and NOGR.

R1

RELS	⟶	RELW	VEGR
			sub (3)
			ord (2)
			aty (0)
			cty (+)
			dty (0)
			ety (0)
			fty (0)
			rty (+)
			omz (+)
			aux

cf. Example 14. p. 123

R1 states that RELS is formed by taking a VEGR of type <u>sub</u> (3) and RELW (relative pronoun).

R2

INFR	————→	FRWO	VEGR sub (1) ord (2) aty (0) cty (+) dty (+) ety (0) fty (0) rty (+) omz (+) aux

cf. Example 12. p. 121

S3

NESA dty (2)	————→	ADVE	VEGR sub (5) ord (2) aty (0) cty (+) dty (+) ety (1) fty (0) rty (+) omz (0) aux

Rule S3 states that a NESA of type <u>dty</u> (2) is formed by taking a VEGR of type <u>sub</u> (5) (infinitive + to) and ADVE.

The nominal group, NOGR

N1	NOGR ⟶	PRÄP	NOGR	für Medizin
N2	NOGR ⟶	ADJE	NOGR	rote Tinte
N3	NOGR ⟶	NOGR	NOGR	ein Schein von Prüfungen
N4	NOGR ⟶	KONJ	NOGR	und Drehbuch
N5	NOGR ⟶	NOGR	RELS	Freund der jetzt studiert
N6	NOGR ⟶	ADVE	NOGR	noch Zeit
N7	NOGR ⟶	NOGR	ADJE	etwas anderes
N8	NOGR ⟶	NOGR	ADVE	der Mann dort

ADVE/ADJE

A1	ADVE ⟶	PRÄP	NOGR	zu Hause
A3	ADJE ⟶	ADJE	NOGR	fertig für den Tag
A4	ADJE ⟶	ADVE	ADJE	so dumm
A5	ADVE ⟶	ADJE	NOGR	jedes Jahr
A7	ADVE ⟶	KONJ	ADVE	und dort
A9	ADVE ⟶	ADVE	ADVE	sehr schnell
A10	ADVE ⟶	ADVE	NESA	dort wo wir wohnen
A12	ADJE ⟶	ADJE	NESA	wichtig die richtige Zeit zu finden

These rules have not been worked out in detail at this level of description in the present study; the above examples roughly show the types of structures involved.

3.9 Probabilistic Weighting of Rules

Probabilities of occurrence must by definition be assigned to a set of alternative events. The events which are of interest here are applications of rules and how their probabilities change during the course of language development.

The probability of an event, E, is often defined as the

$$pr(E) = \frac{\text{number of favourable ways}}{\text{total number of ways}}$$

The probability of rolling an even number with a die, for instance, is 3/6 since three faces of a die have even numbers (2,4,6), i.e. there are three favourable ways, and the total number of ways possible is six. The probabil-

ity of an event that is certain to happen is 1, since the number of favourable ways will equal the total numbers of ways. The probability of an event is therefore a number between 0 and 1.
All possible, mutually exclusive outcomes form the set of alternative events. Since it is certain that with any one trial one event of a given set is bound to happen, the probability associated with all possible outcomes, i.e. with the whole set is 1. The probability of a given set is the sum of the probabilities associated with all outcomes; the probabilities assigned to each element of the set, therefore, add up to 1. Probabilities of occurrence of the basic events of a set need not be equal, and when probabilities cannot be assessed in theory an empirical basis is then required. Suppose a certain event occurs n times in m trials, the ratio n/m is called the relative frequency of the event. After a sufficiently large number of trials n/m will tend towards a certain value, and this value is taken as the empirical probability of occurrence of that event. In the present study the estimated probabilities are the relative frequencies in the application of rules.

In a context-free grammar any group of rules with the same left-hand symbol constitutes a set of alternative events; in the grammar set out above, the left-hand symbol VEGR, for instance, may be re-written in a given number of ways. In the generation of sentences, however, the likelihood of a rule being applied will often depend on the rules preceding it in the derivation. The weighting procedure will, therefore, have to account for such dependencies or constraints in the application of rules. A suitable model was developed by Salomaa (1969) where the transition from a given rule to the next in a derivation is weighted, so that the weightings refer to pairs of rules and not to single occurrences. In order to do this, each rule of the grammar is labelled, r1, r2, r3, etc., and a derivation is represented as a sequence of labelled rules. The set of such sequences as occur is called the "control language" and the sequence of labelled rules associated with a derivation is called the "control word". The "control language" encompasses the set of all the "control words" actually occurring, as opposed to those which are theoretically possible, i.e. could also be generated by the rules of the grammar in question.
In order to ensure that each control word corresponds to one derivation only, the symbols in a derivation are replaced in a fixed order, whereby the left-

most one is replaced first. This is referred to as the "leftmost convention" and is illustrated in the following example:

Tree diagram

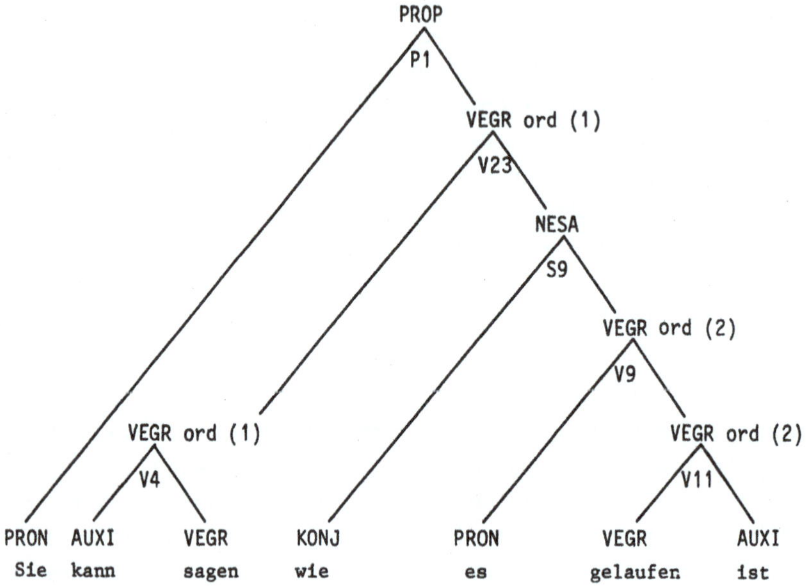

Derivation:

Rules							
	PROP						
P1	PRON	VEGR					
V23	PRON	VEGR	NESA				
V4	PRON	AUXI	VEGR	NESA			
S9	PRON	AUXI	VEGR	KONJ	VEGR		
V9	PRON	AUXI	VEGR	KONJ	PRON	VEGR	
V11	PRON	AUXI	VEGR	KONJ	PRON	VEGR	AUXI
	Sie	kann	sagen	wie	es	gelaufen	ist
	She	can	say	how	it	went	

The first rule PROP ⟶ PRON VEGR is labelled P1, the second VEGR ⟶ VEGR NESA is V23, the third VEGR ⟶ AUXI VEGR is V4 etc. The control word of the derivation is therefore: P1 V23 V4 S9 V9 V11.

Application of the "leftmost convention" in the order of replacement of symbols means that after V23, where VEGR and NESA are available for replacement, the leftmost of the two, VEGR, is replaced before NESA so that V4 precedes S9.

Since the transition from one rule to the next is being weighted and not single occurrences of rules, the above control word consists of the following sequence of transitions or rule pairs:

P1 V23, V23 V4, V4 S9, S9 V9, V9 V11.

Other typical examples of rule pairs occurring in the data are:

P1 V1, V1 V2, V2 A3, A3 A1,
P1 V1, V1 N1,
P1 V2, V2 A3, A3 A1

Rule pairs with the same initial rule (P1 or V1 for example) are drawn together to form a group. Since any of the n rules of the grammar could, in principle, follow any other rule, there are n pair combinations in each group. Each group constitutes a set of alternative events so that the probability values assigned to each event of the group will add up to 1. For instance, in any group with P1 as the initial rule, the probabilities refer to the event that a given rule r_m follows P1. This kind of probabilistic relationship, taking into account all possible groups, is usually represented in matrix form where all the rules of the grammar are listed in the first column and, in the same order, along the top row (see next page) in this matrix the j-th place in the row associated with the rule r_i shows the probability that r_j follows r_i. Many of the cells in the rows associated with each rule are automatically assigned a probability of zero since the grammar does not allow for many of the transitions theoretically possible. 'A' which is the first symbol in the leftmost column is an empty or zero rule which marks the transition probability from no rule to the first rule of the derivation. 'E' at the end of the top row marks the transition from the last rule of the derivation to nothing, i.e. the probability that a derivation ends with a certain rule. The first rule (r_i) of each pair is given in the first column. The probability with which this rule is followed by any of the rules given on the top row (r_j) is given in the row assigned to r_i). The values in each row do not add up to 1 since the table shows only two of the three decimal places calculated.

Transitional Probabilities

IJMR Phase 1 SV

	S3	S4	P1	P4	P7	V24	V1	V2	V3	V4	V5	V6	V9	V10	V11	V13	V15	V16	V18	V19	V21	N1	N2	N3	N4	N5	N6	N7	N8	R1	A1	A3	A4	A7	A9	E
A			.87	.01	.10																															
S3																															1					
S4																			.50									.50								
P1						.01	.50	.15	.16	.01	.01	.03								.03				.01		01										
P4			1																																	
P7						.33	.33					.16												.16												
V24																							.33				.33									.33
V1	.02						.05	.08														.02	.17	.23		11	.05									.20
V2								.25															.06								.43				.18	.06
V3								.10									.10															.20	.50			.10
V4																																				1
V5			1																																	
V6																								.33					.33							.33
V9															.50	.25																				.25
V10																																				1
V11							.33																													.66
V13															1																					
V15																																	1			
V16																																				1
V18																																				1
V19							1																													
V21		1																																		
N1																		.05			.05	.05	.05	11	.05					.05						.52
N2		.05																				.26	.05	05	.10					.05						.42
N3																						.37	.37		.12				.06							.06
N4									.20														.20													.60
N5																							.16	.16						.66						
N6																						.33														.66
N7																						1														
N8																								.50												.50
R1			.16										.66	.16																						
A1																		.09					.09			.09							.18	.09		.45
A3																						.50											.50			
A4																						.10											.10			.80
A7																																				1
A9																															1					

Reading along the first row of the matrix we see that A P1 has a probability of .87. What follows after P1 is shown along the row assigned to P1 (at the fourth position down in the left column), V1 is the most likely rule to follow P1 (P1 V1 .50), (V1 marks an object complement); V2 (an adverbial) follows P1 with a probability of .15, V3 (an adjective) with a probability of .16, and so on. The most probable structure is therefore a subject, consisting of a pronoun (P7 which marks the occurrence of nouns reads .10) followed by a verb which takes an object complement. As the probability values assigned to V1 then show, the object occurs as a complex nominal group (N3) with a probability of .23. Since the reliability of these values depends on the number of occurrences, the absolute values on which the probability is based are given in the matrix below. Here we see, for example, that .23 refers to eight occurrences (V1 N3 in the "absolute values" matrix). Given the range of possibilities present for each point in a derivation, it is obvious that a reliable designation of the probabilities involved requires a large body of data.

In conclusion, a probabilistic Salomaa grammar as defined here consists of a septuple $< V_t, V_n, PROP, R, A, E, p >$ where:

1) $G' = < V_t, V_n, PROP, R >$ is a context-free grammar

2) A and E are arbitrary symbols ($A = r_0$; $E = r_{n+1}$)

3) p is a function which assigns a real value to any element (r_i, r_j) of $\{(R \cup \{A\}), (R \cup \{E\})\}$ such that

   a) for all arguments (r_i, r_j), $p(r_i, r_j) \geq 0$

   b) for all $r \in (R \cup \{A\})$ and all $r_j \in (R \cup \{E\})$

$$\sum_{j=1}^{n+1} p(r, r_j) = 1$$

where n is the number of rules of R.

The function p associates a probability value with each pair, whose first coordinate is either A or a rule, and whose second coordinate is either a rule or E; if n is the number of rules there are $(n + 1)^2$ such pairs.

As mentioned above, this function is represented by a $(n + 1) \cdot (n + 1)$ matrix. The matrix has $(n + 1)^2$ elements $p(r_i, r_j)$. Each element $p(r_i, r_j)$

is written in the intersecting cell of the i-th row and the j-th column and each element $p(r_i, r_j)$ refers to the pair $r_i r_j$.
The transitional probabilities found in this learner language during the phase of development observed are presented in the following chapter.

4. RESULTS

The results presented here describe changes in the structural features of the main sentence types used by the learners over the period of development observed. The main sentence types analysed are as follows:

SV Subject Verb				
PRON	VEGR	NOGR		Er hat viel Angst He has much fear
PRON	VEGR	ADVE		Sie wohnt in der Altstadt She lives in the old town
NOGR	VEGR	ADVE		Die Sonne scheint immer The sun shines always
INV (i): Adverb Verb Subject				
ADVE	VEGR	PRON	ADVE	Dann bleibe ich hier Then remain I here
"	"	"	NOGR	Dann frage ich mein Freund Then ask I my friend
"	"	"	ADJE	Hier ist es schön Here is it nice
INV (ii) Adverb Subject Verb				
ADVE	NOGR	VEGR	ADVE	Jetzt der Wagen fährt schnell Now the car drives fast
SUB (i) Subordinate clauses, verb at end of clause				
KONJ	PRON	NOGR	VEGR	Wenn wir die Scheine bekommen Wenn we the credits receive
"	"	ADVE	"	Weil wir hier bleiben Because we here stay
"	"	ADJE	"	... daß er gut ist ... that he good is
SUB (ii) Subordinate clauses, verb not at end of clause				
KONJ	PRON	VEGR	NOGR etc.	Weil wir sehen die Stadt Because we see the town

AUXI	Subj. Auxiliary	——	Verb	
PRON	AUXI	NOGR	VEGR	Sie hat die Stadt besichtigt She has the town toured
"	"	ADVE	"	Er ist nach Hause gefahren He is home gone
INV + AUXI				
ADVE	AUXI	PRON	NOGR etc.	Heute haben sie eine Sammlung gehabt Today have they a collection had

Interrogative and imperative clauses were excluded in this analysis due to the low number of occurrences. SV and AUXI comprise sentence types with the finite verb in second position; in AUXI this is an auxiliary or modal verb while the participle or infinitive is generally placed at the end of the sentence.
INV and INV + AUXI are sentences with an adverbial phrase or simple adverb in the initial position followed by an inversion of the subject verb sequence. INV (ii) is similar to this group except that no inversion of the subject verb sequence occurs.

SUB (i) refers to subordinate clauses introduced by KONJ (conjunctions) in which the verb is placed in the final position in the clause. SUB (ii) comprises subordinate clauses in which the verb does not appear in the final position but has a main clause constituent order.
Table 1 shows the relative frequency of the above sentence types over the nine weeks of development observed. Phase I refers to data collected in conversations held during the first two weeks of the period of observation, II refers to the third and fourth week, III refers to the sixth and seventh week and IV refers to the eight and ninth week.
Karin's data were analysed separately since she was at a slightly more advanced stage of development. All data were pooled in INV and SUB, however, on account of the very low number of occurrences.

Tab. 1: Relative frequency of sentence types over the nine weeks of development observed

	PHASE I	PHASE II	PHASE III	PHASE IV
SV	.42	.35	.36	.36
INV*	.08	.08	.07	.12
SUB	.13	.21	.22	.12
AUXI	.22	.22	.22	.22
INV + AUXI	.10	.07	.05	.05

*INV(i) and (ii) and SUB (i) and (ii) are pooled here

As the values here illustrate, this period of development is not marked by distinct changes on the sentence level; the changes occur most markedly at the constituent level. Each sentence type was analysed separately and the pattern of development found in each case will be presented in detail in the following.

In order to account for interdependencies in the application of rules which mark features of development this analysis is based on computations of the probability of a given rule being applied in conjunction with the one preceding it in the derivation. The relative frequency with which pairs of rules were found to occur are interpreted here as probabilities; the possible range of values lies between 0 and 1. The principles of the weighting procedure followed were discussed above and will not be treated again here. The probabilities obtained are set out in matrix form for each of the sentence types analysed and read as follows (see Table SV, p. 52).

The first rule of each pair r_n is placed in the first <u>column</u> of the matrix, the second rule in the top <u>row</u>. The probability with which the second rule (r_m) follows the first (r_n) is placed in the row beside r_n. Consider Table SV, p. 52. For example, P1 (forth rule down in the first column) is followed by V1 (seventh rule on top row) with a probability of .50 during Phase I, i.e. the first two weeks of the observation. Nine weeks later (see Table SV, p. 56) the probability that P1 is followed by V1 has dropped to .32.

P1 labels the rule PROP ⟶ PRON VEGR, V1 VEGR ⟶ VEGR NOGR (cf. p. 24). These rules generate teh string PRON VEGR NOGR, i.e. a subject, verb, object sentence.

IJMR

Phase 1 SV

Transitional Probabilities

	S3	S4	P1	P4	P7	V24	V1	V2	V3	V4	V5	V6	V9	V10	V11	V13	V15	V16	V18	V19	V21	N1	N2	N3	N4	N5	N6	N7	N8	R1	A1	A3	A4	A7	A9	E
A			.87	.01	.10																															
S3																															1					
S4																			.50									.50								
P1						.01	.50	.15	.16	.01	.01	.03								.03				.01		01										
P4			1																																	
P7						.33	.33					.16												.16												
V24																							.33				.33									.33
V1	.02						.05	.08														.02	.17	.23		11	.05									.20
V2								.25															.06								.43				.18	.06
V3								.10									.10															.20	.50			.10
V4																																				1
V5			1																																	
V6																								.33					.33							.33
V9															.50	.25																				.25
V10																																				1
V11							.33																													.66
V13															1																					
V15																																	1			
V16																																				1
V18																																				1
V19							1																													
V21		1																																		
N1																		.05			.05	.05	.05	11	.05					.05						.52
N2		.05																				.26	.05	05	.10					.05						.42
N3																						.37	.37		.12				.06							.06
N4									.20														.20													.60
N5																							.16	.16						.66						
N6																						.33														.66
N7																						1														
N8																								.50												.50
R1			.16										.66	.16																						
A1																		.09					.09			.09							.18	.09		.45
A3																						.50											.50			
A4																						.10											.10			.80
A7																																				1
A9																															1					

IJMR Phase 1 SV Absolute Values

	S3	S4	P1	P4	P7	V24	V1	V2	V3	V4	V5	V6	V9	V10	V11	V13	V15	V16	V18	V19	V21	N1	N2	N3	N4	N5	N6	N7	N8	R1	A1	A3	A4	A7	A9	E
A	.	.	50	1	6	.	.	.	.	.	.	.	.	.	.	.	.	.	.	.	.	.	.	.	.	.	.	.	.	.	.	.	.	.	.	.
S3	.	.	.	.	.	.	.	.	.	.	.	.	.	.	.	.	.	.	.	.	.	.	.	.	.	.	.	.	.	.	1	.	.	.	.	.
S4	.	.	.	.	.	.	.	.	.	.	.	.	.	.	.	.	.	.	1	.	.	.	.	.	.	.	.	1	.	.	.	.	.	.	.	.
P1	.	.	.	.	.	1	27	8	9	1	1	2	.	.	.	.	.	.	.	2	.	.	.	1	.	1	.	.	.	.	.	.	.	.	.	.
P4	.	.	1	.	.	.	.	.	.	.	.	.	.	.	.	.	.	.	.	.	.	.	.	.	.	.	.	.	.	.	.	.	.	.	.	.
P7	.	.	.	.	.	2	2	.	.	.	.	1	.	.	.	.	.	.	.	.	.	.	.	1	.	.	.	.	.	.	.	.	.	.	.	.
V24	.	.	.	.	.	.	.	.	.	.	.	.	.	.	.	.	.	.	.	.	.	.	1	.	.	.	1	.	.	.	.	.	.	.	.	1
V1	1	.	.	.	.	.	2	3	.	.	.	.	.	.	.	.	.	.	.	.	.	1	6	8	.	4	2	.	.	.	.	.	.	.	.	7
V2	.	.	.	.	.	.	.	4	.	.	.	.	.	.	.	.	.	.	.	.	.	.	1	.	.	.	.	.	.	.	7	.	.	.	3	1
V3	.	.	.	.	.	.	.	1	.	.	.	.	.	.	.	.	1	.	.	.	.	.	.	.	.	.	.	.	.	.	.	2	5	.	.	1
V4	.	.	.	.	.	.	.	.	.	.	.	.	.	.	.	.	.	.	.	.	.	.	.	.	.	.	.	.	.	.	.	.	.	.	.	1
V5	.	.	1	.	.	.	.	.	.	.	.	.	.	.	.	.	.	.	.	.	.	.	.	.	.	.	.	.	.	.	.	.	.	.	.	.
V6	.	.	.	.	.	.	.	.	.	.	.	.	.	.	.	.	.	.	.	.	.	.	.	1	.	.	.	.	1	.	.	.	.	.	.	1
V9	.	.	.	.	.	.	.	.	.	.	.	.	.	.	2	1	.	.	.	.	.	.	.	.	.	.	.	.	.	.	.	.	.	.	.	1
V10	.	.	.	.	.	.	.	.	.	.	.	.	.	.	.	.	.	.	.	.	.	.	.	.	.	.	.	.	.	.	.	.	.	.	.	1
V11	.	.	.	.	.	.	1	.	.	.	.	.	.	.	.	.	.	.	.	.	.	.	.	.	.	.	.	.	.	.	.	.	.	.	.	2
V13	.	.	.	.	.	.	.	.	.	.	.	.	.	.	1	.	.	.	.	.	.	.	.	.	.	.	.	.	.	.	.	.	.	.	.	.
V15	.	.	.	.	.	.	.	.	.	.	.	.	.	.	.	.	.	.	.	.	.	.	.	.	.	.	.	.	.	.	.	.	1	.	.	.
V16	.	.	.	.	.	.	.	.	.	.	.	.	.	.	.	.	.	.	.	.	.	.	.	.	.	.	.	.	.	.	.	.	.	.	.	2
V18	.	.	.	.	.	.	.	.	.	.	.	.	.	.	.	.	.	.	.	.	.	.	.	.	.	.	.	.	.	.	.	.	.	.	.	1
V19	.	.	.	.	.	.	2	.	.	.	.	.	.	.	.	.	.	.	.	.	.	.	.	.	.	.	.	.	.	.	.	.	.	.	.	.
V21	.	1	.	.	.	.	.	.	.	.	.	.	.	.	.	.	.	.	.	.	.	.	.	.	.	.	.	.	.	.	.	.	.	.	.	.
N1	.	.	.	.	.	.	.	.	.	.	.	.	.	.	.	.	.	1	.	.	1	1	1	2	1	.	.	.	.	1	.	.	.	.	.	9
N2	.	1	.	.	.	.	.	.	.	.	.	.	.	.	.	.	.	.	.	.	.	5	1	1	2	.	.	.	.	1	.	.	.	.	.	8
N3	.	.	.	.	.	.	.	.	.	.	.	.	.	.	.	.	.	.	.	.	.	6	6	.	2	.	.	.	1	.	.	.	.	.	.	1
N4	.	.	.	.	.	.	.	.	1	.	.	.	.	.	.	.	.	.	.	.	.	.	1	.	.	.	.	.	.	.	.	.	.	.	.	3
N5	.	.	.	.	.	.	.	.	.	.	.	.	.	.	.	.	.	.	.	.	.	.	1	1	.	.	.	.	.	4	.	.	.	.	.	.
N6	.	.	.	.	.	.	.	.	.	.	.	.	.	.	.	.	.	.	.	.	.	1	.	.	.	.	.	.	.	.	.	.	.	.	.	2
N7	.	.	.	.	.	.	.	.	.	.	.	.	.	.	.	.	.	.	.	.	.	1	.	.	.	.	.	.	.	.	.	.	.	.	.	.
N8	.	.	.	.	.	.	.	.	.	.	.	.	.	.	.	.	.	.	.	.	.	.	.	1	.	.	.	.	.	.	.	.	.	.	.	1
R1	.	.	1	.	.	.	.	.	.	.	.	.	4	1	.	.	.	.	.	.	.	.	.	.	.	.	.	.	.	.	.	.	.	.	.	.
A1	.	.	.	.	.	.	.	.	.	.	.	.	.	.	.	.	.	1	.	.	.	.	1	.	.	1	.	.	.	.	.	.	2	1	.	5
A3	.	.	.	.	.	.	.	.	.	.	.	.	.	.	.	.	.	.	.	.	.	1	.	.	.	.	.	.	.	.	.	.	1	.	.	.
A4	.	.	.	.	.	.	.	.	.	.	.	.	.	.	.	.	.	.	.	.	.	1	.	.	.	.	.	.	.	.	.	.	1	.	.	8
A7	.	.	.	.	.	.	.	.	.	.	.	.	.	.	.	.	.	.	.	.	.	.	.	.	.	.	.	.	.	.	.	.	.	.	.	1
A9	.	.	.	.	.	.	.	.	.	.	.	.	.	.	.	.	.	.	.	.	.	.	.	.	.	.	.	.	.	.	3	.	.	.	.	.

IJMR Phase 2 SV

Transitional Probabilities

	S3	S4	P1	P7	V1	V2	V3	V6	V8	V9	V10	V12	V16	V19	V20	V21	N1	N2	N3	N4	N5	N6	N7	N8	R1	A3	A4	A5	A9	E
A			.90	.09																										
S3																													.50	
S4													.66				.33													
P1					.36	.16	.22	.04	.02	.02				.08	.02	.02			.04											
P7					.40	.20	.20											.20												
V1	.03	.03				.21											.10	.14	.10		.03	.10		.03						.14
V2					.09	.19	.04	.04										.04	.04		.04				.04			.04	.09	.04
V3																										23	.38			.38
V6		.25																	.25				.25							.25
V8						1																								
V9												.50																		.50
V10																														.33
V12																														1
V16																														1
V19					.75			.25																						
V20						1																								
V21	1																													
N1					.12								.06				.06	.06	.12								.06			.50
N2			.08		.08																									83
N3																	.41	.08	.16	.16	.08	.08								
N4																									.50					.50
N5																	.25	.25				.25			.25					
N6																	.16	.16							.16					.50
N7																											1			
N8		1																												
R1										.25	.75																			
A1													.10					.20	.10		.10	.10								.40
A3																	1													
A4																	.14													.85
A5													.50																	.50
A9																												.33		.33

IJMR Phase 2 SV

Absolute Values

	S3	S4	P1	P7	V1	V2	V3	V6	V8	V9	V10	V12	V16	V19	V20	V21	N1	N2	N3	N4	N5	N6	N7	N8	R1	A1	A3	A4	A5	A9	E
A			43	5																											
S3																										1				1	
S4													2				1														
P1					18	8	11	2	1	1				4	1	1			2												
P7					2	1	1											1													
V1	1	1				6											3	4	3		1	3		1		1					4
V2					2	4	1	1										1	1		1				1	5			1	2	1
V3																											3	5			5
V6		1																	1				1								1
V8						1																									
V9												1																			1
V10																										2					1
V12																															1
V16																															5
V19					3			1																							
V20						1																									
V21	1																														
N1					2								1				1	1	2									1			8
N2			1		1																										10
N3																	5	1	2	2	1	1									
N4																									1						1
N5																	1	1				1			1						
N6																	1	1							1						3
N7																												1			
N8		1																													
R1										1	3																				
A1													1					2	1		1	1									4
A3																	3														
A4																	1														6
A5													1																		1
A9																										1			1		1

Transitional Probabilities

IJMR Phase 3 SV

	S1	P1	P7	V26	V1	V2	V3	V6	V8	V9	V10	V11	V12	V13	V20	N1	N2	N3	N5	N6	N8	R1	A1	R2	A3	A4	A9	E
A		.92	.07																									
S1										1																		
P1					.36	.30	.24	.02	.04						.02			.02										
P7							.75											.25										
V26											1																	
V1					.04	.18											.18	.04	.09	.09	.04		.04					.27
V2					.06	.25		.09				.03											.22				.03	.29
V3													.06		.06										.06	18		.62
V6																		.25										.75
V8						1																						
V9				.50																								.50
V10														.33									.33					.33
V11																												1
V12	1																											
V13												1																
V20					.50																	.50						
N1							.16									.16	.16					.16						.33
N2																	.10							.10				.80
N3						.20										.40				.20								.20
N5																		.50				.50						
N6																.66					.33							
N8																	.50											.50
R1										.33	.66																	
A1												.11					.33											.55
R2						1																						
A3																1												
A4																												1
A9																												1

Absolute Values

IJMR Phase 3 SV

	S1	P1	P7	V26	V1	V2	V3	V6	V8	V9	V10	V11	V12	V13	V20	N1	N2	N3	N5	N6	N8	R1	A1	R2	A3	A4	A9	E
A		50	4																									
S1										1																		
P1					18	15	12	1	2						1			1										
P7							3											1										
V26											1																	
V1					1	4											4	1	2	2	1		1					6
V2					2	8		3				1											7				1	9
V3													1		1										1	3		10
V6																		1										3
V8						2																						
V9				1																								1
V10														1									1					1
V11																												3
V12	1																											
V13												1																
V20					1																	1						
N1							1									1	1					1						2
N2																	1							1				8
N3						1										2				1								1
N5																		1				1						
N6																2					1							
N8																	1											1
R1										1	2																	
A1												1					3											5
R2						1																						
A3																1												
A4																												3
A9																												1

IJMR Phase 4 SV Transitional Probabilities

	S3	P1	P7	V24	V1	V2	V3	V6	V8	V9	V11	V16	V20	N1	N2	N3	N4	N5	N6	R1	A1	A3	A4	A5	A12	A9	E
A		.76	.23																								
S3																										1	
P1					.32	.24	.26		.10				.02			.04											
P7					.13	.13	.33		.06						.13	.20											
V24																			1								
V1					.04	.28								.08	.04	.04	.04	.08	.12								.28
V2						.12		.09						.06		.03				.03	.31			.03		.09	.21
V3					.05																	.15	.42				.36
V6																					.33					66	
V8					.66	.16																					.16
V9											.50				.50												
V11																											1
V16																											1
V20						1																					
N1				.06	06									.06	.18												.62
N2						.18								.09						.09							.63
N3						.11	.11							.44	.11	.11	.11										
N4						.50																					.50
N5																			.50	.50							
N6														.40	.40												.20
R1						.33				.66																	
A1												.06		.06	.06	.06											.73
A3														.33									.66				
A4														.20											.10		.70
A5																					.50						.50
A12	1																										
A9																					.42			.14		14	.28

IJMR Phase 4 SV Absolute Values

	S3	P1	P7	V24	V1	V2	V3	V6	V8	V9	V11	V16	V20	N1	N2	N3	N4	N5	N6	R1	A1	A3	A4	A5	A12	A9	E
A		49	15																								
S3																										1	
P1					16	12	13		5				1			2											
P7					2	2	5		1						2	3											
V24																			1								
V1					1	7								2	1	1	1	2	3								7
V2						4		3						2		1				1	10			1		3	7
V3					1																	3	8				7
V6																					1					2	
V8					4	1																					1
V9											1				1												
V11																											1
V16																											1
V20						1																					
N1				1	1									1	3												10
N2						2								1						1							7
N3						1	1							4	1	1	1										
N4						1																					1
N5																			1	1							
N6														2	2												1
R1						1				2																	
A1												1		1	1	1											11
A3														1									2				
A4														2											1		7
A5																					1						1
A12	1																										
A9																					3			1		1	2

4.1 The Sentence Type SV

The three main categories occurring in predicative position in sentences of this type are adverbs and nominal phrases with adverbial function, ADVE; adjectives, ADJE, which are mainly simple;and pronouns and nominal phrases, NOGR,with object function. Changes in probability of occurrence of these three categories are set out below. These values are taken from the matrices on pages 52 to 56.

		Transitional probabilities			
Final string	Rule pairs	I	II	III	IV
PRON VEGR NOGR	P1 V1	.50	.36	.36	.32
PRON VEGR ADVE	P1 V2	.15	.16	.30	.24
PRON VEGR ADJE	P1 V3	.16	.32	24	.26

Phases I and II are marked by a dominance of NOGR in predicative position. By Phase IV this dominance has been replaced by closer probabilities for all categories.

Subject position

The following word classes occur in this position with markedly different probabilities:

	Phases			
word class	I	II	III	IV
prounouns	.87	.90	.92	.76
nouns and nominal phrases	.10	.09	.07	.23

Nouns in subject position are marked by occurrences of the rule P7; the relevant transitional probabilities are given in the matrices under P7 on row A (A indicates the probability with which the various P-rules initiate the derivations). Occurrences of nouns in subject position are very low prior to Phase IV. The absolute occurrences range from 6 sentences in Phase I, 5 in Phase II to 4 in Phase III. This word class is not applied systematically in production in this position until Phase IV when occurrences increase to fifteen sentences.

Constituents appearing in predicative position with <u>nouns</u> in subject pos.		
Predicative position	Rule pairs	Phase IV
NOGR (obj.)	P7 V1	.13
ADVE	P7 V2	.13
ADJE	P7 V3	.33

As the distribution of values in phase IV indicates, the application of nouns in subject position is accompanied by a dominance of ADJE and ADVE in predicative position and not of NOGR. This pattern of development will be taken up again below.

SV comprises both copular sentences and sentences with finite verbs. These two groups of sentences were subsequently analysed separately since copular sentences indicated a different pattern of development. The pattern of development in predicative and subject position in sentence type SV is now presented without copular sentences.

Pattern of development in SV without copular sentences

Predicative position

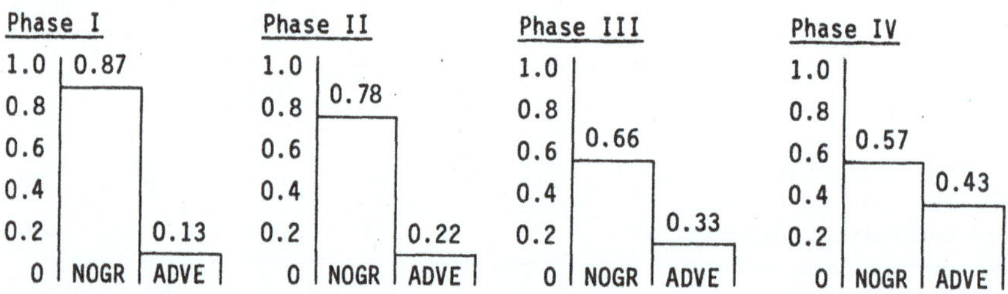

Subject position

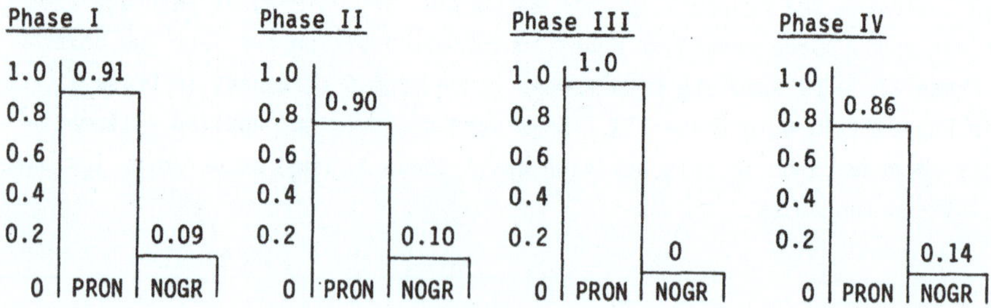

Pronouns and nominal phrases NOGR with object function occur with a probability of .87 in Phase I, decreasing to .57 in Phase IV. ADVE increases from .13 in Phase I to .43 in Phase IV.

In subject position the dominance of pronouns over nouns is .91 in Phase I and decreases only marginally to .86 in Phase IV.

A further feature of development is represented by changes in the complexity of categories occurring in predicative position. This is marked by the pairs of rules V1 E, V2 E and V3 E where E represents the end of a derivation. V1 E shows that the NOGR generated by this rule is not expanded as any expansion would appear as V1 N; the same case applies to adverbials (V2 A) and adjectives V3 A. Categories appearing in predicative position decrease in complexity over the four phases analysed as the following values show (indicated by an increase in the probability of E being preceded by V1, V2 and V3 respectively).

Pair	Phases I	II	III	IV
V1 E	0.20	0.14	0.27	0.28
V2 E	0.06	0.04	0.29	0.21
V3 E	0.10	0.38	0.62	0.36

This tendency is also reflected in the decreasing number of actual expansions of these categories, i.e. the probability with which V1 is followed by rules generating complex NOGR-phrases, or V2 by rules generating complex adverbials etc.

	Phases I	II	III	IV
V1 - NOGR-Rules	0.58	0.53	0.44	0.40
V2 - ADVE-Rules	0.62	0.42	0.25	0.43
V3 - ADJE-Rules	0.70	0.61	0.24	0.57

These values were obtained by summing the probabilities of all N-rules, adverbial and adjectival rules in the rows following V1, V2 and V3 respectively in the matrices I - IV (pages 52 to 56). However, all expansions of categories do not immediately succeed the rule generating them as a result of the "leftmost convention" in the expansion of rules in strings (cf. p. 45). N2 in the row V2 in the matrix SV (p. 52) describes a structure generated by V1 and not V2. Where expansions of categories are of interest this case should be included in those following V1. Since the probabilities expressed on row V2 bear no relation to those on V1, calculations should be made on the basis of the absolute number of occurrences given in the matrix directly below.

This decrease in the complexity of categories in predicative position is accompanied by an increase in the number of categories occurring in this position, as reflected in the increased probability of V1 being followed by V2, i.e. structures such as

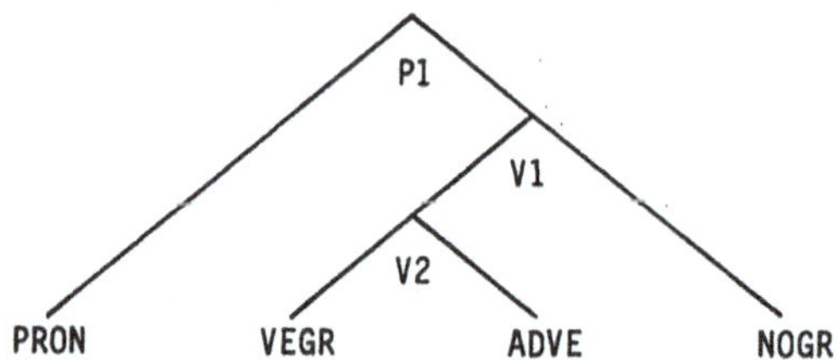

Phases	I	II	III	IV
V1 V2	.08	.21	.25	.28

Summary

Patterns of development observed in sentences of this type (SV) can be summarised as follows: Pronouns constitute the dominant word class in subject position during the period of development observed, this dominance of pronouns in subject position is coupled in the initial stages observed with a dominance of pronouns and nouns with object function(NOGR) in predicative position, which decreases steadily during Phase III and IV. In Phase IV NOGR and ADVE (adverbs and adverbial phrases) approach equal probability of occurrence in predicative position.

An increase in the use of nouns in subject position which emerges towards the end of this period of observation is coupled with a dominance of adjectives

and adverbials in predicative position and not with nouns and noun phrases (NOGR).
Categories occurring in predicative position, NOGR and ADVE, become less complex over the four phases of development observed. This decrease in complexity is accompanied by an increase in the number of categories occurring in sentences, i.e. PRON VEGR ADVE NOGR now emerges beside PRON VEGR NOGR and PRON VEGR ADVE.

As shown above, development in speech production is marked not so much by the presence or absence of specific structures but by changes in distribution or dominance over time. The frame of reference is therefore changing probabilities of occurrence which requires a statistically adequate data base.
The subsequent sentence types analysed do not occur with frequencies comparable to the group presented so far (SV) so that the results presented in the following are tentative.

4.2 Sentences with a Copula

The number of copular sentences occurring in the data is low so that it is not possible to present definite patterns of development.
Simple nouns, noun phrases and adjectives appear with equal probability in predicative position while nouns in subject position increase in frequency in Phases III and IV. This emergence of simple nouns and nominal phrases in subject position is coupled with a dominance of ADJE in predicative position. The following combination of categories seem to hold in sentences of this type at this stage of development.

Subject position | Predicative position

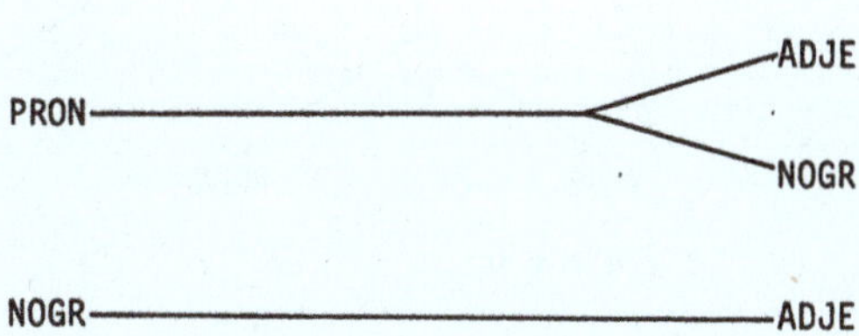

This pattern of development indicates that such restrictions on the occurrences of rules are a reflection of principles governing the process of development in speech production and need not directly reflect the organisation of the underlying system. It is unlikely that certain structural features have to be re-learned during later stages of development, that speakers would have to re-learn, that nouns and noun phrases can occur in predicative position when nouns emerge in subject position.

4.3 The Sentence Type INV

This sentence type is also low in number in comparison to SV with no more than 13 sentences in Phase I, increasing to 25 in Phase IV. Sentences of this type are either followed by an inversion of the subject verb sequence, as required in German, or not. The former structures are generated by the PROP-rule P2, the latter by P3.

The absolute values for these two sequences over the four phases are as follows:

	I	II	III	IV
P2	13	19	13	25
P3	7	10	6	8

The following examples illustrate the type of structures analysed here.

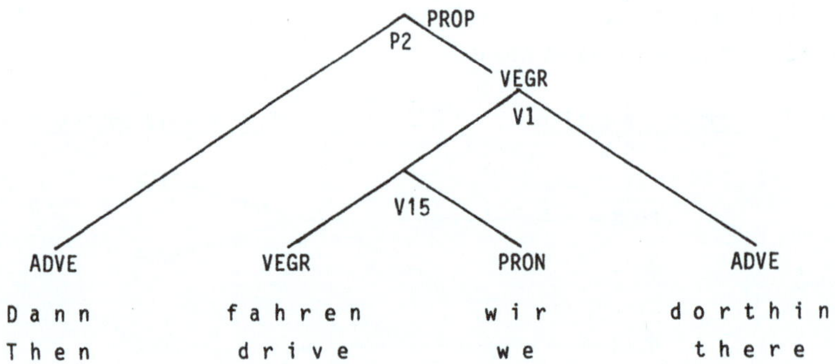

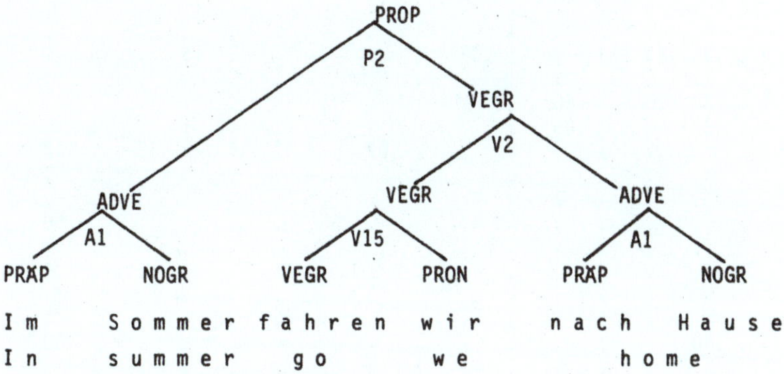

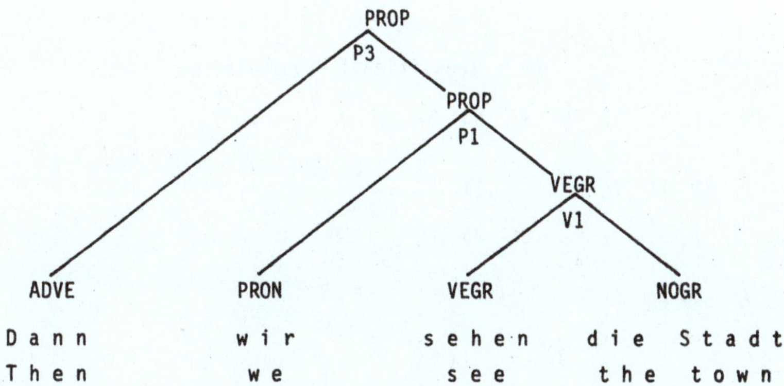

P3 describes structures with an adverbial in initial position and non-inversion of the subject verb sequence. These show a somewhat different pattern of development than sentences with subject verb inversion (P2). This is illustrated by the probabilities with which the following pairs of rules P2 V1, P2 V2 and P1 V1 occur in the respective sets of data (see matrices given on pages 64 to 67).

IJKMR Ph. I INV P2 Transitional Probabilities

	S4	P2	V1	V2	V3	V15	V16	V19	N1	N2	N3	N6	N7	A1	A3	A5	E
A	.	1	.	.	.	.	.	.	.	.	.	.	.	.	.	.	.
S4	.	.	.	.	.	.	1	.	.	.	.	.	.	.	.	.	.
P2	.	.	.15	.23	.23	.	.	.07	.	.	.	.	.	.15	.	.15	.
V1	.	.	.	.	.	1	.	.	.	.	.	.	.	.	.	.	.
V2	.	.	.20	.20	.	.60	.	.	.	.	.	.	.	.	.	.	.
V3	.	.	.33	.	.	.66	.	.	.	.	.	.	.	.	.	.	.
V15	.07	.	.	.	.	.	.	.	.	.07	.	.07	.15	.23	.15	.	.23
V16	.	.	.	.	.	.	.	.	.	.	.	.	.	.	.	.	1
V19	.	.	.	.	.	1	.	.	.	.	.	.	.	.	.	.	.
N1	.	.	.	.	.	.	.	.	.	.	.50	.	.	.	.	.	.50
N2	.	.	.	.	.	.	.	.	.	.	.	.	.	.	.	.	1
N3	.	.	.	.	.	.	.	.	.	.	.	.	.	.	.	.	1
N6	.	.	.	.	.	.	.	.	.	1	.	.	.	.	.	.	.
N7	.	.	.	.	.	.	.	.	.	.	.	.	.	.	.	.	1
A1	.	.	.40	.	.	.	.	.	.	.	.	.	.	.	.	.	.60
A3	.	.	.	.	.	.	.	.	1	.	.	.	.	.	.	.	.
A5	.	.	.	.50	.	.50	.	.	.	.	.	.	.	.	.	.	.

IJKMR Ph.I P3 Transitional Probabilities

	P1	P3	V1	V2	V3	N1	N2	N3	N7	A1	E
A	.	1	.	.	.	.	.	.	.	.	.
P1	.	.	.57	.14	.14	.	.	.14	.	.	.
P3	.85	.	.	.	.	.	.	.	.	.14	.
V1	.	.	.	.	.	.	.25	.25	.25	.	.25
V2	.	.	.	.	.	.	.	.	.	.50	.50
V3	.	.	.	.	.	.	.	.	.	.	1
N1	.	.	.	.50	.	.	.50	.	.	.	.
N2	.	.	.	.	.	.	.	.	.	.	1
N3	.	.	.	.	.	1	.	.	.	.	.
N7	.	.	.	.	.	.	.	.	.	.	1
A1	.50	.	.	.	.	.	.	.	.	.	.50

The first rule (r_m) of each pair is given in the first column. The probability with which this rule is followed by any of the rules appearing on the top row (r_n) is given in the row following r_m. Row A shows the first rule in the derivation, column E the last.

IJKMR Ph.II INV P2 Transitional Probabilities

	P2	V1	V2	V3	V9	V10	V15	N1	N2	N3	N5	N6	R1	A1	A3	A4	A5	E
A	1	.	.	.	.	.	.	.	.	.	.	.	.	.	.	.	.	.
P2	.	.26	.21	.10	.	.	.10	.	.	.	.	.	.	.21	.	.	.10	.
V1	.	.	.	.	.	.	.85	.	.	.14	.	.	.	.	.	.	.	.
V2	.	.	.33	.	.	.	.66	.	.	.	.	.	.	.	.	.	.	.
V3	.	.	.	.	.	.	1	.	.	.	.	.	.	.	.	.	.	.
V9	.	.	.	.	.	1	.	.	.	.	.	.	.	.	.	.	.	.
V10	.	.	.	.	.	.	.	.	.	.	.	.	.	1	.	.	.	.
V15	.	.	.	.	.	.	.	.	.05	.11	.	.11	.	.16	.05	.11	.	.38
N1	.	.	.	.	.	.	.	.	.	.	.	.	.	.	.	.	.	1
N2	.	.	.	.20	.	.	.	.20	.	.	.	.	.	.	.	.	.	.60
N3	.	.	.	.25	.	.	.	.25	.25	.	.	.25	.	.	.	.	.	.
N5	.	.	.	.	.	.	.	.	.	.	.	.	1	.	.	.	.	.
N6	.	.	.	.	.	.	.	.	.66	.	.	.	.	.	.	.	.	.33
R1	.	.	.	.	1	.	.	.	.	.	.	.	.	.	.	.	.	.
A1	.	.25	.	.12	.	.	.	.	.12	.	.12	.	.	.	.	.	.	.37
A3	.	.	.	.	.	.	.	1	.	.	.	.	.	.	.	.	.	.
A4	.	.	.	.	.	.	.	.	.	.	.	.	.	.	.	.	.	1
A5	.	.	.	.50	.	.	.	.	.	.50	.	.	.	.	.	.	.	.

IJKMR Ph.II P3 Transitional Probabilities

	P1	P3	V1	V2	V3	V9	V11	V13	N1	N2	N3	N5	N6	N8	R1	A1	E
A	.	1	.	.	.	.	.	.	.	.	.	.	.	.	.	.	.
P1	.	.	.50	.20	.20	.	.	.	.	.	.	.	.	.10	.	.	.
P3	.40	.	.	.	.	.	.	.	.	.	.	.	.	.	.	.60	.
V1	.	.	.	.	.	.	.	.	.14	.	.28	.14	.14	.	.	.	.28
V2	.	.	.33	.33	.	.	.	.	.	.	.	.	.	.	.	.33	.
V3	.	.	.	.	.	.	.	.	.	.	.	.	.	.	.	.	1
V9	.	.	.	.	.	.	.	1	.	.	.	.	.	.	.	.	.
V11	.	.	.	.	.	.	.	.	.	.	.	.	.	.	.	.	1
V13	.	.	.	.	.	.	1	.	.	.	.	.	.	.	.	.	.
N1	.	.	.	.	.	.	.	.	.	.	.	.	.	.	.	.	1
N2	.	.	.	.	.	.	.	.	.50	.	.	.	.	.	.50	.	.
N3	.	.	.	.	.	.	.	.	.50	.	.	.	.50	.	.	.	.
N5	.	.	.	.	.	.	.	.	.	1	.	.	.	.	.	.	.
N6	.	.	.	.	.	.	.	.	.	.50	.	.	.	.	.	.50	.
N8	.	.	1	.	.	.	.	.	.	.	.	.	.	.	.	.	.
R1	.	.	.	.	.	1	.	.	.	.	.	.	.	.	.	.	.
A1	.75	.	.	.	.	.	.	.	.	.	.	.	.	.	.	.	.25

IJKMR Ph. III INV P2 Transitional Probabilities

	P2	V1	V2	V3	V6	V8	V15	V16	N1	N2	N3	N6	N7	A2	A4	E
A	1	.	.	.	.	.	.	.	.	.	.	.	.	.	.	.
P2	.	.38	.30	.15	.07	.07	.	.	.	.	.	.	.	.	.	.
V1	.	.	.11	.	.	.	.77	.	.	.	.	.	.	.	.	.11
V2	.	.50	.	.	.	.	.50	.	.	.	.	.	.	.	.	.
V3	.	.	.	.	.	.	1	.	.	.	.	.	.	.	.	.
V6	.	.	1	.	.	.	.	.	.	.	.	.	.	.	.	.
V8	.	1	.	.	.	.	.	.	.	.	.	.	.	.	.	.
V15	.	.	.	.	.	.	.	.	.	.16	.08	.08	.08	.08	.08	.41
V16	.	.	.	.	.	.	.	.	.	.	.	.	.	.	.	1
N1	.	.	.	.	.	.	.	.33	.	.	.	.	.	.	.	.66
N2	.	.	.	.	.	.	.	.	.33	.	.33	.	.	.	.	.33
N3	.	.	.	.	.	.	.	.	.	.50	.	.	.	.	.	.50
N6	.	.	.	.	.	.	.	.	1	.	.	.	.	.	.	.
N7	.	.	.	.	.	.	.	.	.	.	.	.	.	.	.	1
A2	.	.	.	.	.	.	.	.	1	.	.	.	.	.	.	.
A4	.	.	.	.	.	.	.	.	.	.	.	.	.	.	.	1

IJKMR Ph.III P3 Transitional Probabilities

	P1	P3	V1	V2	V3	V7	N2	N3	N4	N7	A1	A4	A5	E
A	.	1	.	.	.	.	.	.	.	.	.	.	.	.
P1	.	.	.33	.	.16	.	.16	.16	.	.	.	.	.	.16
P3	.50	.	.	.	.	.	.	.	.	.	.33	.	.16	.
V1	.	.	.	.	.	.	.	.50	.	.50	.	.	.	.
V2	.	.	.	.	.	.50	.	.	.	.	.50	.	.	.
V3	.	.	.	.	.	.	.	.	.	.	.	1	.	.
V7	.	.	.	.	.	.	.	.	.	.	1	.	.	.
N2	.	.	.	1	.	.	.	.	.	.	.	.	.	.
N3	.	.	.	.	.	.	.	.	.50	.	.	.	.	.50
N4	.	.	.	1	.	.	.	.	.	.	.	.	.	.
N7	.	.	.	.	.	.	.	.	.	.	.	.	.	1
A1	.50	.	.	.	.	.	.	.	.	.	.	.	.	.50
A4	.	.	.	.	.	.	.	.	.	.	.	.	.	1
A5	1	.	.	.	.	.	.	.	.	.	.	.	.	.

IJKMR Ph.IV INV P2 Transitional Probabilities

	P2	V1	V2	V3	V15	V17	N1	N2	N6	A1	A5	A9	E
A	1	.	.	.	.	.	.	.	.	.	.	.	.
P2	.	.36	.28	.08	.12	.	.	.	.	.08	.08	.	.
V1	.	.	.08	.	.83	.	.	.	.	.	.	.	.08
V2	.	.20	.	.	.70	.	.	.	.	.	.	.10	.
V3	.	.	.	.	1	.	.	.	.	.	.	.	.
V15	.	.	.	.	.	.04	.04	.08	.04	.04	.	.08	.65
V17	.	.	.	.	.	.	.	1	.	.	.	.	.
N1	.	.	.	.	.	.	.	.	.	.	.	.	1
N2	.	.	.	.	.	.	.	.	.	.25	.	.	.75
N6	.	.	.	.	.	.	.	1	.	.	.	.	.
A1	.	.	.33	.	.	.	.	.	.	.	.	.	.66
A5	.	.50	.	.	.50	.	.	.	.	.	.	.	.
A9	.	.	.	.	.	.	.	.	.	.66	.	.	.33

IJKMR Ph.IV P3 Transitional Probabilities

	P1	P3	V1	V2	V3	V11	N2	N3	N5	N6	N8	R1	A1	A4	A5	E
A	.	1	.	.	.	.	.	.	.	.	.	.	.	.	.	.
P1	.	.	.75	.12	.12	.	.	.	.	.	.	.	.	.	.	.
P3	.50	.	.	.	.	.	.	.	.	.	.	.	.37	.	.12	.
V1	.	.	.	.	.	.	.	.16	.16	.50	.	.	.	.	.	.16
V2	.	.	.	.	.	.	.	.	.	.	.	.	.	.	.	1
V3	.	.	.	.	.	.	.	.	.	.	.	.	.	1	.	.
V11	.	.	.	.	.	.	.	.	.	.	.	.	.	.	.	1
N2	.50	.	.	.	.	.	.	.	.	.	.	.	.	.	.	.50
N3	.	.	.	.	.	.	.	.	.	.	1	.	.	.	.	.
N5	.	.	.	.	.	.	.	.	.	.	.	1	.	.	.	.
N6	.	.	.	.	.	.	.33	.	.	.	.	.	.	.	.	.66
N8	.	.	.	.	.	.	.	.	.	.	.	.	.	.	.	1
R1	.	.	.	.	.	1	.	.	.	.	.	.	.	.	.	.
A1	1	.	.	.	.	.	.	.	.	.	.	.	.	.	.	.
A4	.	.	.	.	.	.	.	.	.	.	.	.	.	.50	.	.50
A5	.	.	.	.	.	.	1	.	.	.	.	.	.	.	.	.

Pairs	+Inversion		I	II	III	IV
P2 V1		NOGR	.15	.26	.38	.36
P2 V2		ADVE	.23	.21	.30	.28
P2 V3		ADJE	.23	.10	.15	.08
	-Inversion					
P1 V1		NOGR	.57	.50	.33	.75
P1 V2		ADVE	.14	.20	.32*	.12
P1 V3		ADJE	.14	.20	.16	.12

Sentences without inversion of the subject verb sequence show a pattern of development similar to that observed in SV. The predicative position is marked by a dominance of nouns and noun phrases[6] (NOGR) while this does not apply in structures described by P2 (inversion of the subject verb sequence following an adverb). Here adverbials and adjectives dominate up to Phase IV, while Phases I to III show an increase in the use of NOGR in predicative position. In spite of the low frequency of occurrence, an overall tendency is nevertheless discernible.

The pattern of development in sentences with inversion of the subject verb sequence is characterised by a decrease in the use of adverbials and adjectives and an increase in the occurrence of nouns and nominal phrases. The latter reach a level of application in Phase IV similar to that observed in the early stages of development in sentence type SV. This sequence indicates that earlier stages of development may be characterised by a dominance of adverbials and adjectives in predicative position.
In German, sentences with adverbs in the initial position in the sentence are followed by inversion of the subject verb sequence. In this learner language, approximately half the sentences of this type are formed without inversion of the subject verb sequence. Whether inversion occurs or not seems to be associated with two factors: the complexity of the adverb in the initial position and the occurrence of nouns and noun phrases with object function in predicative position.

---

[6]With the exception of Phase III however; such fluctuations can be expected with low numbers of samples.

*This value includes the N2-V2, N3-V2 transitions

As the following probabilities show complex adverbs are more likely to follow P3 (non-inversion) than P2.

	Phases			
	I	II	III	IV
P2 + complex ADVE	.30	.31	-	.16
P3 + complex ADVE	.14	.60	.49	.49

It would seem that when the adverb is complex learners tend to apply the more familiar SV sequence. Furthermore, nouns and nominal phrases with object function are more likely to occur in conjunction with P3 (non-inversion) than P2.

	Phases			
Pairs	I	II	III	IV
P2 V1	.15	.26	.38	.36
P3 V1	.57	.50	.33	.75

When nouns and nominal phrases with object function (as opposed to adverbial) appear in predicative position inversion of the subject verb sequence is less likely to occur. We see that simple adverbs in sentence initial position and adverbials in predicate position enhance the likelihood of occurrence of subject verb inversion. In the encoding process this means that the nature of the syntactic category that appears <u>after</u> the subject verb position determines what happens at the subject position, thus indicating that the <u>syntactic</u> categories occurring in the sentence, the nature of the verb complements etc., are determined before the surface structure form is selected.
As with SV, the categories occurring in predicative position also decrease in complexity during the four phases observed. This is marked by the increasing probability with which E, which marks the end of the derivation, follows V15.

Pairs	I	II	III	IV
V15 E	.23	.38	.41	.65

However, this decrease in complexity is not accompanied by any increase in the number of categories occurring in sentences of this type.

Pairs		I	II	III	IV
V2 V2	ADVE ADVE	.20	.33	-	.10
V2 V1	ADVE NOGR	.20	-	.50	.20
V1 V2	NOGR ADVE	-	-	.11	.08
VI V1	NOGR NOGR	-	-	-	-

Summary

Development within sentence types with adverbs in the initial position (INV) is marked by a dominance of adverbials and adjectives during the early stages. A dominance of nouns and and nominal phrases with object function first occurs in Phase IV. This sequence points to a pattern of development where a dominance of adverbials and adjectives is later replaced by a period of object dominance. Approximately half of the sentences of this type are not followed by inversion of the subject verb sequence. Inversion of the subject verb sequence, as is required in German, is less likely to occur if the initial adverb is complex and/or if objects occur in predicative position. This shows that certain contexts tend to enhance application of emerging structures.

4.4 Subordinate clauses

Subordinate clauses introduced by conjunctions are at first infrequent in number. The subsequent increase in occurrence, however, permits observation of features of development holding at stages preceding those observed with simple sentences (SV). Adverbial clauses constitute the most frequent clause type during the initial stages of development. The following table shows their probability of occurrence in clauses with the verb in final position (cf. matrices p. 77 to 80).

Clause	Rule	Type	Phases			
			I	II	III	IV
wenn	S5	adv.	.76	.68	.64	.42
weil	S7	adv.	.19	.10	.11	.20
daß	S1	obj.	.04	.21	.17	.22
wie	S9	obj.	.0	0	.05	.14

<u>wenn</u>: if/when; <u>weil</u>: because; <u>daß</u>: that; <u>wie</u>: how

Sub-clauses show two constituent order patterns: the finite verb is placed either at the end of the clause (sub), as is required in German, or appears in second position as in main clauses (m.cl.). The following table shows the probability with which these constituent orders occur with respect to clause type:

Clause	Order	Phases			
		I	II	III	IV
wenn	sub	.67	.35	.42	.33
	m.cl.	.12	0	.02	.02
weil	sub	.16	.05	.08	.15
	m.cl.	0	.32	.12	.11
daß	sub	.04	.11	.12	.18
	m.cl.	0	.16	.20	.15
wie	(both)	(0	0	.02	.04)

Verb-final position is more likely to occur in <u>wenn</u>-clauses than in <u>weil</u>- or <u>daß</u>-clauses. This factor will be discussed in detail below. The internal structure of clauses with a finite verb in the final position will be presented first. The following example illustrates the type of structure referred to here.

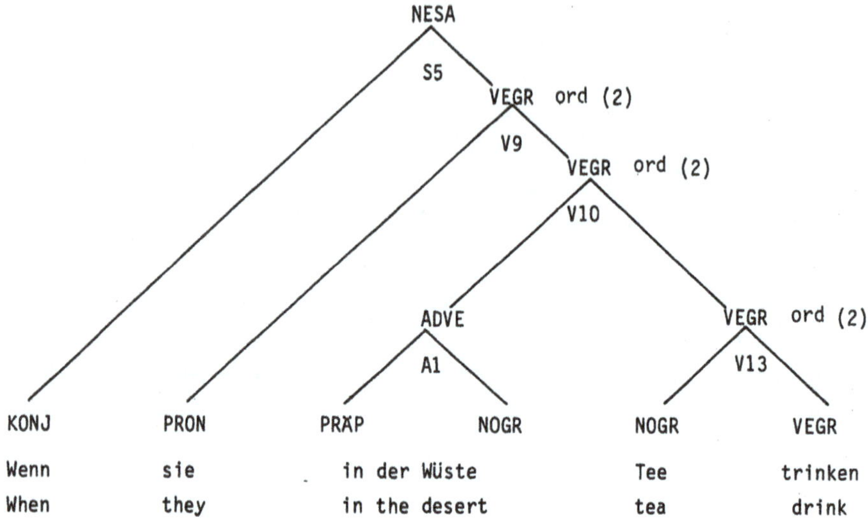

In these derivations V9 which generates the subject pronoun (or V25 if the subject consists of a noun or noun phrase) follows the 'S' rule. The transitional probabilities given on row V9 (see matrix p.77) refer therefore to structures occurring between the subject of the clause and the finite verb. As is evident from the example given above, V9 transitions present only an indirect indication of the complexity of the structures occurring in this position. Transitions such as V10 V13, i.e. ADVE followed by NOGR, V13 V10 or A-V13 have also to be taken into account. V9 transitions are useful as a general indicator, however, since the clause structure is still simple.

Pairs		Phases			
		I	II	III	IV
V9 V10	ADVE	.42	.57	.47	.33
V9 V12	ADJE	.19	.15	.11	.16
V9 V13	NOGR	.28	.26	.32	.33

In phases I, II and III ADVE has the highest probability of occurrence decreasing only in phase IV while NOGR increases marginally over this period to reach a similar probability of occurrence in IV. As in sentences with inversion of the subject verb sequence (INV) simple adverbs and nominal phrases with adverbial function (ADVE as well as ADJE) have a higher probability of occurrence initially than nouns and nominal phrases with object function (NOGR). The decrease in the application of adverbs and adverbial phrases with an accompanying increase in the use of nouns and nominal phrases with object function indicates that the period of dominance of ADVE is being replaced by that of NOGR. NOGR dominance was observed in main clauses with simple finite verbs in second position (SV).

The adverbial structure generated by V10 may consist of a simple adverb, <u>here there</u> etc., or a prepositional phrase of varying complexity. These are generated by the appropriate A-rules (see p. 45). Complex object phrases are generated by N-rules. The following table shows which of the above categories ADVE, NOGR and ADJE are likely to consist of complex structures. The values are taken from the matrices on pages 77 to 80 . All V10-A transition probabilities on row V10 such as V10, A1, V10, A2 were added together and compared with the corresponding V13-N and V12-A transitions (i.e. A rules generating adjectival phrases).

Pairs	Complex Phrases	Phases			
		I	II	III	IV
V10 - AV	ADVE	.27	.49	.66	.52
V13 - N	NOGR	.16	0	.27	.08
V12 - AJ	ADJE	.25	.66	.25	.28

The dominant category ADVE is also the most complex of the three in overall terms and reaches a peak in complexity in Phase III. NOGR remains simple during the first two phases. The values under NOGR and ADJE are based on very low absolute occurrences (cf. matrices) and are therefore less reliable than ADVE. A comparision with the complexity of categories in simple sentences (SV) is nevertheless informative as an indicator of the general pattern of development.

SV	Phases			
	I	II	III	IV
V1 N -	.58	.50	.44	.40
V2 AV -	.62	.36	.25	.43
V3 AJ -	.70	.61	.24	.57

The sentence type SV is marked by a dominance of NOGR during this period of development. As opposed to the pattern presented in subordinate clauses, the non-dominant categories, i.e. ADVE and ADJE, are nevertheless equally as complex as NOGR. This further indicates that the period of dominance of NOGR in SV may have been preceded by a period of dominance of adverbial and adjectival phrases.

According to the results presented in the table below, wenn clauses are more likely to be formed with the finite verb in the final position in the clause, as required in German, than weil or daß clauses (because or that). As will be shown in the following the application of the rule placing the verb in the final position of the clause correlates with two factors: the complexity of the clause, measured in terms of the number of main constituents, and the syntactic function of the clause, i.e. adverbial or object. The subordinate clauses were grouped according to the number of main constituents and the following table shows the probability with which the finite verb occurs in the final or main clause position.

Clause	Position of verb	4 main constituents	5 main constituents
adv.	final	.92	.74
wenn	main cl.	.08	.26
adv.	final	.67	.20
weil	main cl.	.33	.80
obj.	final	.57	.36
daß	main cl.	.43	.64

The complexity factor can be seen to apply in all three cases; simple clauses show a higher incidence of target-like structures (final position) than more complex ones. This demonstrates that the application of knowledge of the language during speech production is affected by attentional factors, i.e. the amount of processing capacity available for the execution of the different tasks which speech production involves. When the complexity of the task exceeds the capacity available the speaker is forced to draw on structures which are more highly automated, which in this case are SV sequences.

This corresponds to the observation made earlier in the discussion of sentences with introductory adverbs (INV), which in German require inversion of the subject verb sequence. If the initial adverbial consists of a complex nominal phrase (as opposed to a simple adverb such as here, there) inversion of the subject verb sequence is less likely to occur (cf. p. 68). Here it can also be argued that the complexity of the task exceeds the learner's capacity and application of the inversion rule is inhibited. The learner again reverts to a more highly automated sequence of constituents.

The second factor seen to influence application of the rule placing the verb at the end of the subordinate clause is the order of appearance of syntactic categories. As the results presented so far indicate, structures with adverbial function are applied before those with object function. In clauses with four main constituents both adverbial clause types, wenn and weil, show a higher incidence of target-like structures (verb in final position) than clauses with object function (daß). This sequence, however, is not upheld in clauses with five main constituents, here daß clauses show a higher incidence of target like structures than weil- clauses. There is no ready explanation for this shift. Differences between wenn and weil could be attributed to the learner's attentional span or planning capacity: wenn clauses generally precede the matrix sentence which means that the more difficult structure, taken in developmental terms, is produced first. Weil, on the other hand, generally follows the matrix sentence. In terms of unit length daß clauses are simpler than weil since daß is embedded in what are usually simple SV structures - "ich sehe daß ...". The higher number of target-like structures in weil clauses with four constituents can therefore be attributed to the overall pattern of development in production. However, none of these factors serves to explain the shift of position of weil-clauses with respect to daß when the former has five main constituents. This shift may also be attributable to the fact that in spoken German the finite verb in weil-clauses is often placed after the subject and not in final position.

Summary

Subordinate clauses show two constituent order patterns; the finite verb is placed either at the end of the clause, as required in German, or appears in another position, i.e. following the subject of the clause. Adverbial clauses show a higher incidence of target-like structures (verb in the final position) than clauses with object function. The internal structure of clauses where verbs are placed in the final position is marked by a dominance of adverbs and adverbial phrases during the first phases of observation. ADVE dominance decreases in Phase IV while NOGR increases steadily over the entire period to reach a probability of occurrence similar to that of ADVE in Phase IV, thus indicating that the period of dominance of ADVE is being replaced by that of NOGR. In other words, subordinate clauses are reaching a stage of development in Phase IV (weeks eight and nine of the period of observation) similar to that exhibited in simple sentences (SV) in Phase I. Such successive periods of dominance indicate that learners focus on different sets of syntactic relations in turn while learning to implement their knowledge of the second language during communication.
Each new sentence type is subject to the same learning focus or pattern of dominance; a simple transfer of 'learning' across contexts does not occur. At a certain point in development nouns with object function can appear in main clauses but not, as yet, in subordinate clauses.
The application of the rule placing the verb in the final position in the clause correlates with two factors: the complexity of the clause and the order of dominance or learning focus. In adverbial clauses, for instance, the verb is more likely to be placed in the final position in sequences with 4 constituents than those with 5. The application of knowledge during speech production is therefore affected by attentional factors, i.e. the amount of processing capacity allocated to the execution of the tasks involved. When the complexity of the task exceeds the capacity available the learner reverts to a more highly automated structure, such as SV sequences.

IJKMR Ph.I SUB Transitional Probabilities

	S1	S5	S7	V3	V9	V10	V11	V12	V13	N6	A1	A4	E
A	.04	.76	.19	.	.	.	.	.	.	.	.	.	.
S1	.	.	.	.	1	.	.	.	.	.	.	.	.
S5	.	.	.	.	1	.	.	.	.	.	.	.	.
S7	.	.	.	.	1	.	.	.	.	.	.	.	.
V3	.	.	.	.	.	.	.	.	.	.	.	.	1
V9	.	.	.	.04	.	.42	.04	.19	.28	.	.	.	.
V10	.	.	.	.	.	.18	.	.	.	.	.27	.	.54
V11	.	.	.	.	.	.	.	.	.	.	.	.	1
V12	.	.	.	.	.	.	.	.	.	.	.	.25	.75
V13	.	.	.	.	.	.	.16	.	.	.16	.	.	.66
N6	.	.	.	.	.	.	1	.	.	.	.	.	.
A1	.	.	.	.	.	.	.	.	.	.	.	.	1
A4	.	.	.	.	.	.	.	.	.	.	.	.	1

IJKMR Ph.I SUB Absolute values

	S1	S5	S7	V3	V9	V10	V11	V12	V13	N6	A1	A4	E
A	1	16	4	.	.	.	.	.	.	.	.	.	.
S1	.	.	.	.	1	.	.	.	.	.	.	.	.
S5	.	.	.	.	16	.	.	.	.	.	.	.	.
S7	.	.	.	.	4	.	.	.	.	.	.	.	.
V3	.	.	.	.	.	.	.	.	.	.	.	.	1
V9	.	.	.	1	.	9	1	4	6	.	.	.	.
V10	.	.	.	.	.	2	.	.	.	.	3	.	6
V11	.	.	.	.	.	.	.	.	.	.	.	.	3
V12	.	.	.	.	.	.	.	.	.	.	.	1	3
V13	.	.	.	.	.	.	1	.	.	1	.	.	4
N6	.	.	.	.	.	.	1	.	.	.	.	.	.
A1	.	.	.	.	.	.	.	.	.	.	.	.	3
A4	.	.	.	.	.	.	.	.	.	.	.	.	1

IJKMR Ph.II SUB Transitional Probabilities

	S1	S5	S7	V9	V10	V11	V12	V13	A1	A3	A4	A9	E
A	.21	.68	.10	.	.	.	.	.	.	.	.	.	.
S1	.	.	.	1	.	.	.	.	.	.	.	.	.
S5	.	.	.	1	.	.	.	.	.	.	.	.	.
S7	.	.	.	1	.	.	.	.	.	.	.	.	.
V9	.	.	.	.	.57	.	.15	.26	.	.	.	.	.
V10	.	.	.	.	.	.08	.	.08	.33	.08	.	.16	.25
V11	.	.	.	.	.	.	.	.	.	.	.	.	1
V12	.	.	.	.	.	.	.	.	.	.	.66	.	.33
V13	.	.	.	.	.16	.16	.	.	.	.	.	.	.66
A1	.	.	.	.	.	.60	.	.	.	.	.	.	.40
A3	.	.	.	.	.	1	.	.	.	.	.	.	.
A4	.	.	.	.	.	.	.	.	.	.	.	.	1
A9	.	.	.	.	.	.	.	.	.50	.	.	.	.50

IJKMR Ph.II SUB Absolute values

	S1	S5	S7	V9	V10	V11	V12	V13	A1	A3	A4	A9	E
A	4	13	2	.	.	.	.	.	.	.	.	.	.
S1	.	.	.	4	.	.	.	.	.	.	.	.	.
S5	.	.	.	13	.	.	.	.	.	.	.	.	.
S7	.	.	.	2	.	.	.	.	.	.	.	.	.
V9	.	.	.	.	11	.	3	5	.	.	.	.	.
V10	.	.	.	.	.	1	.	1	4	1	.	2	3
V11	.	.	.	.	.	.	.	.	.	.	.	.	6
V12	.	.	.	.	.	.	.	.	.	.	2	.	1
V13	.	.	.	.	1	1	.	.	.	.	.	.	4
A1	.	.	.	.	.	3	.	.	.	.	.	.	2
A3	.	.	.	.	.	1	.	.	.	.	.	.	.
A4	.	.	.	.	.	.	.	.	.	.	.	.	2
A9	.	.	.	.	.	.	.	.	1	.	.	.	1

IJKMR Ph.III SUB Transitional Probabilities

	S1	S5	S7	V9	V10	V11	V12	V13	N2	N6	S9	A1	A4	A9	E
A	.17	.64	.11	.	.	.	.	.	.	.	.05	.	.	.	.
S1	.	.	.	1	.	.	.	.	.	.	.	.	.	.	.
S5	.	.	.	1	.	.	.	.	.	.	.	.	.	.	.
S7	.	.	.	1	.	.	.	.	.	.	.	.	.	.	.
V9	.	.	.	.	.47	.02	.11	.32	.	.	.	.	.	.	.05
V10	.	.	.	.	.	.09	.	.	.	.	.	.47	.	.19	.23
V11	.	.	.	.	.	.	.	.	.	.	.	.	.	.	1
V12	.	.	.	.	.	.	.	.	.	.	.	.	.25	.	.75
V13	.	.	.	.	.27	.18	.	.	.09	.18	.	.	.	.	.27
N2	.	.	.	.	.	.	.	.	.33	.	.	.	.	.	.66
N6	.	.	.	.	.	1	.	.	.	.	.	.	.	.	.
S9	.	.	.	1	.	.	.	.	.	.	.	.	.	.	.
A1	.	.	.	.	.	.40	.	.	.10	.	.	.	.	.	.50
A4	.	.	.	.	.	.	.	.	.	.	.	.	.	.	1
A9	.	.	.	.	.50	.50	.	.	.	.	.	.	.	.	.

IJKMR Ph.III SUB Absolute values

	S1	S5	S7	V9	V10	V11	V12	V13	N2	N6	S9	A1	A4	A9	E
A	6	22	4	.	.	.	.	.	.	.	2	.	.	.	.
S1	.	.	.	6	.	.	.	.	.	.	.	.	.	.	.
S5	.	.	.	22	.	.	.	.	.	.	.	.	.	.	.
S7	.	.	.	4	.	.	.	.	.	.	.	.	.	.	.
V9	.	.	.	.	16	1	4	11	.	.	.	.	.	.	2
V10	.	.	.	.	.	2	.	.	.	.	.	10	.	4	5
V11	.	.	.	.	.	.	.	.	.	.	.	.	.	.	13
V12	.	.	.	.	.	.	.	.	.	.	.	.	1	.	3
V13	.	.	.	.	3	2	.	.	1	2	.	.	.	.	3
N2	.	.	.	.	.	.	.	.	1	.	.	.	.	.	2
N6	.	.	.	.	.	2	.	.	.	.	.	.	.	.	.
S9	.	.	.	2	.	.	.	.	.	.	.	.	.	.	.
A1	.	.	.	.	.	4	.	.	1	.	.	.	.	.	5
A4	.	.	.	.	.	.	.	.	.	.	.	.	.	.	1
A9	.	.	.	.	2	2	.	.	.	.	.	.	.	.	.

IJKMR Ph.IV SUB Transitional Probabilities

	S1	S5	S7	V2	V9	V10	V11	V12	V13	N1	N3	N7	S9	A1	A4	A5	A9	E
A	.22	.42	.20	.	.	.	.	.	.	.	.	.	.14	.	.	.	.	.
S1	.	.	.	.	1	.	.	.	.	.	.	.	.	.	.	.	.	.
S5	.	.	.	.	1	.	.	.	.	.	.	.	.	.	.	.	.	.
S7	.	.	.	.	1	.	.	.	.	.	.	.	.	.	.	.	.	.
V2	.	.	.	.	.	.	.	.	.	.	.	.	.	.	1	.	.	.
V9	.	.	.	.02	.02	.33	.	.16	.33	.	.	.02	.	.	.	.	.	.08
V10	.	.	.	.	.	.	.26	.	.	.	.	.	.	.20	.	.06	.26	.20
V11	.	.	.	.	.	.	.	.	.	.	.	.	.	.	.	.	.	1
V12	.	.	.	.	.14	.	.	.	.	.	.	.	.	.	.28	.	.	.57
V13	.	.	.	.	.	.16	.25	.	.	.	.08	.	.	.	.	.	.	.50
N1	.	.	.	.	.	.	.	.	.	.	.	.	.	.	.	.	.	1
N3	.	.	.	.	.	.	.	.	.	1	.	.	.	.	.	.	.	.
N7	.	.	.	.	.	.	.	.	.	.	.	.	.	.	.	.	.	1
S9	.	.	.	.	.80	.	.	.20	.	.	.	.	.	.	.	.	.	.
A1	.	.	.	.	.	.	.	.	.	.	.	.	.	.	.	.	.	1
A4	.	.	.	.	.	.	.33	.	.	.	.	.	.	.	.	.	.	.66
A5	.	.	.	.	.	.50	.	.	.	.	.	.	.	.	.	.	.	.50
A9	.	.	.	.	.	.	.	.	.	.	.	.	.	.50	.	.25	.	.25

IJKMR Ph.IV SUB Absolute values

	S1	S5	S7	V2	V9	V10	V11	V12	V13	N1	N3	N7	S9	A1	A4	A5	A9	E
A	8	15	7	.	.	.	.	.	.	.	.	.	5	.	.	.	.	.
S1	.	.	.	.	8	.	.	.	.	.	.	.	.	.	.	.	.	.
S5	.	.	.	.	15	.	.	.	.	.	.	.	.	.	.	.	.	.
S7	.	.	.	.	7	.	.	.	.	.	.	.	.	.	.	.	.	.
V2	.	.	.	.	.	.	.	.	.	.	.	.	.	.	1	.	.	.
V9	.	.	.	1	1	12	.	6	12	.	.	1	.	.	.	.	.	3
V10	.	.	.	.	.	.	4	.	.	.	.	.	.	3	.	1	4	3
V11	.	.	.	.	.	.	.	.	.	.	.	.	.	.	.	.	.	8
V12	.	.	.	.	1	.	.	.	.	.	.	.	.	.	2	.	.	4
V13	.	.	.	.	.	2	3	.	.	.	1	.	.	.	.	.	.	6
N1	.	.	.	.	.	.	.	.	.	.	.	.	.	.	.	.	.	1
N3	.	.	.	.	.	.	.	.	.	1	.	.	.	.	.	.	.	.
N7	.	.	.	.	.	.	.	.	.	.	.	.	.	.	.	.	.	1
S9	.	.	.	.	4	.	.	1	.	.	.	.	.	.	.	.	.	.
A1	.	.	.	.	.	.	.	.	.	.	.	.	.	.	.	.	.	5
A4	.	.	.	.	.	.	1	.	.	.	.	.	.	.	.	.	.	2
A5	.	.	.	.	.	1	.	.	.	.	.	.	.	.	.	.	.	1
A9	.	.	.	.	.	.	.	.	.	.	.	.	.	2	.	1	.	1

4.5 The Sentence Type AUXI

The pattern of development here is similar to that observed in SV.

	Phases			
Predicative position	I	II	III	IV
NOGR	.57	.62	.60	.42
ADVE	.38	.29	.28	.42

Phases I to III show a dominance of nouns and nominal phrases with object function which decreases markedly in Phase IV. As in SV this is accompanied with an increase in the occurrence of ADVE (cf. matrices on pages 82, 83).

	Phases			
Subject position	I	II	III	IV
Pronouns	1	.95	.93	.92
Nouns and nominal phrases	0	.05	.06	.07

The pattern observed here is similar to that in SV except that here pronoun dominance, though diminishing, is still high in Phase IV. In SV nouns had reached a probability of occurrence of .23 in IV. These values indicate that this sentence type (AUXI) is slightly behind SV in order of development in second language production.

Features of development in sentence type INV + AUXI were not analysed in detail due to their low frequency of occurrence.

AUXI Phase I Transitional Probabilities

	S3	S4	P1	P4	P5	V1	V4	V9	V10	V11	V14	V16	V17	V18	V19	V20	V22	N1	N2	N3	N6	R1	A1	A5	A7	A9	E
A	.	.	.88	.07	.02	.	.	.02	.	.	.	.	.	.	.	.	.	.	.	.	.	.	.	.	.	.	.
S3	.	.	.	.	.	.	.	.	.	.	.	.50	.	.50	.	.	.	.	.	.	.	.	.	.	.	.	.
S4	.	.	.	.	.	.	.	.	.	.	.	1	.	.	.	.	.	.	.	.	.	.	.	.	.	.	.
P1	.	.	.	.	.	.	.95	.	.	.	.	.	.	.	.04	.	.	.	.	.	.	.	.	.	.	.	.
P4	.	.	1	.	.	.	.	.	.	.	.	.	.	.	.	.	.	.	.	.	.	.	.	.	.	.	.
P5	.	.	1	.	.	.	.	.	.	.	.	.	.	.	.	.	.	.	.	.	.	.	.	.	.	.	.
V1	.	.	.	.	.	.	.	.	.	.	.	.	.	.	.	.	.	.	1	.	.	.	.	.	.	.	.
V4	.	.	.	.	.	.	.	.	.	.	.02	.	.30	.32	.02	.02	.27	.	.	.	.	.	.02	.	.	.	.
V9	.	.	.	.	.	.	.	.	.50	.50	.	.	.	.	.	.	.	.	.	.	.	.	.	.	.	.	.
V10	.	.	.	.	.	.	.	.50	.	.	.	.	.	.	.	.	.	.	.	.	.	.	.	.	.	.	.
V11	.	.	.	.	.	.	.	.	.	.	.	.	.	.	.	.	.	.	.	.	.	.	.	.	.	.	.50
V14	.	.	.	.	.	.	.	.	.	.	.	.	.	.	.	.	.	.	.	.	.	.	.	.	.	.	1
V16	.	.	.	.	.	.	.	.	.	.	.	.	.	.	.	.	.	.	.	.	.	.	.	.	.	.	1
V17	.	.07	.	.	.	.	.	.	.	.	.	.	.	.28	.	.	.	.07	.	.	.07	.	.07	.	.	.	.42
V18	.03	.	.	.	.	.	.	.	.	.	.	.	.03	.07	.	.	.03	.	.	.	.	.	.23	.15	.	.26	.15
V19	.	.	.	.	.	.33	.33	.	.	.	.	.	.33	.	.	.	.	.	.	.	.	.	.	.	.	.	.
V20	.	.	.	.	.	.	.	.	.	.	.	.	.	1	.	.	.	.	.	.	.	.	.	.	.	.	.
V22	.	.	.	.	.	.	.	.	.	.	.	.	.	.07	.	.	.	.07	.15	.15	.07	.	.	.	.	.	.46
N1	.	.	.	.	.	.	.	.	.	.	.	.	.	.20	.	.	.	.	.	.	.	.	.	.	.	.	.80
N2	.20	.	.	.	.	.	.	.	.	.	.	.	.	.	.	.	.	.20	.	.	.	.	.	.	.20	.	.40
N3	.	.	.	.	.	.	.	.	.	.	.	.	.	.	.	.	.	.33	.33	.	.	.	.	.	.	.	.33
N6	.	.	.	.	.	.	.	.	.	.	.	.50	.	.	.	.	.	.50	.	.	.	.	.	.	.	.	.
R1	.	.	.	.	.	.	.	.	1	.	.	.	.	.	.	.	.	.	.	.	.	.	.	.	.	.	.
A1	.	.	.	.	.	.	.	.	.	.	.	.	.	.16	.	.	.	.	.08	.08	.	.	.	.	.08	.	.58
A5	.	.	.	.	.	.	.	.	.	.	.	.	.	.25	.	.	.	.	.	.	.	.	.	.	.	.	.75
A7	.	.	.	.	.	.	.	.	.	.	.	.	.	.	.	.	.50	.	.	.	.	.	.	.	.	.	.50
A9	.	.	.	.	.	.	.	.	.	.	.	.	.	.	.	.	.	.	.	.	.	.14	.57	.	.	.	.28

AUXI Phase II Transitional Probabilities

	P1	P4	P5	P7	V4	V14	V17	V18	V22	N1	N2	N3	N6	N7	A1	A4	A5	A9	V28	V29	E
A	.87	.05	.02	.05	.	.	.	.	.	.	.	.	.	.	.	.	.	.	.	.	.
P1	.	.	.	.	.91	.	.	.	.	.	.05	.02	.	.	.	.	.	.	.	.	.
P4	.50	.	.	.50	.	.	.	.	.	.	.	.	.	.	.	.	.	.	.	.	.
P5	1	.	.	.	.	.	.	.	.	.	.	.	.	.	.	.	.	.	.	.	.
P7	.	.	.	.	.66	.	.	.	.	.	.33	.	.	.	.	.	.	.	.	.	.
V4	.	.	.	.	.	.02	.22	.35	.27	.	.	.	.	.	.	.	.	.	.02	.07	.02
V14	.	.	.	.	.	.	.	.	.	.	.	.	.	.	.	1	.	.	.	.	.
V17	.	.	.	.	.	.	.	.22	.11	.	.22	.11	.	.11	.	.	.	.	.	.	.22
V18	.	.	.	.	.	.	.	.04	.09	.	.	.	.	.	.38	.	.04	.04	.	.04	.33
V22	.	.	.	.	.	.	.	.20	.06	.13	.13	.06	.06	.	.	.	.	.	.	.	.33
N1	.	.	.	.	.	.	.	.	.	.	.25	.	.	.	.	.	.	.	.	.	.75
N2	.	.	.	.	.40	.	.	.	.	.10	.	.	.	.	.	.	.	.	.	.	.50
N3	.	.	.	.	.	.	.	.	.	.75	.	.	.25	.	.	.	.	.	.	.	.
N6	.	.	.	.	.	.	.	.	.	.66	.	.	.	.	.33	.	.	.	.	.	.
N7	.	.	.	.	.	.	.	1	.	.	.	.	.	.	.	.	.	.	.	.	.
A1	.	.	.	.	.	.	.	.	.	.	.11	.11	.	.	.	.	.	.	.	.	.77
A4	.	.	.	.	.	.	.	.	.	.	.	.	.	.	.	.	.	.	.	.	1
A5	.	.	.	.	.	.	.	.	.	.	.	.	.	.	.	.	.	.	.	.	1
A9	.	.	.	.	.	.	.	.	.	.	.	.	.	.	.	.	.	.	.	.	1
V28	.	.	.	.	.	.	.	.	.	.	.	.	.	.	.	.	.	.	.	.	1
V29	.	.	.	.	.	.	.	.	.	.	.	.	.25	.	.	.	.	.	.	.	.75

AUXI Phase III Transitional Probabilities

	P1	P4	P7	V4	V8	V9	V10	V11	V17	V18	V20	V22	N1	N2	N3	N6	R1	A1	A3	A5	A7	A9	V28	V29	E
A	.84	.07	.07	.	.	.	.	.	.	.	.	.	.	.	.	.	.	.	.	.	.	.	.	.	.
P1	.	.	.	.97	.	.	.	.	.	.	.02	.	.	.	.	.	.	.	.	.	.	.	.	.	.
P4	1	.	.	.	.	.	.	.	.	.	.	.	.	.	.	.	.	.	.	.	.	.	.	.	.
P7	.	.	.	.66	.	.	.	.	.	.	.	.	.	.33	.	.	.	.	.	.	.	.	.	.	.
V4	.	.	.	.	.02	.	.	.	.26	.36	.	.23	.	.	.	.	.	.	.	.	.	.	.02	.	.07
V8	.	.	.	.	.	.	.	.	.	.	.	.	.	.	.	.	.	1	.	.	.	.	.	.	.
V9	.	.	.	.	.	.	1	.	.	.	.	.	.	.	.	.	.	.	.	.	.	.	.	.	.
V10	.	.	.	.	.	.	.	1	.	.	.	.	.	.	.	.	.	.	.	.	.	.	.	.	.
V11	.	.	.	.	.	.	.	.	.	.	.	.	.	.	.	.	.	.	.	.	.	.	.	.	1
V17	.	.	.	.	.	.	.	.	.07	.30	.	.	.07	.	.	.	.07	.	.	.	.	.	.	.	.46
V18	.	.	.	.	.	.	.	.	.03	.15	.	.11	.	.	.	.	.	.19	.03	.07	.	.03	.	.03	.30
V20	.	.	.	1	.	.	.	.	.	.	.	.	.	.	.	.	.	.	.	.	.	.	.	.	.
V22	.	.	.	.	.	.	.	.	.07	.23	.	.	.	.15	.07	.07	.	.07	.	.	.	.	.	.	.30
N1	.	.	.	.	.	.	.	.	.	.	.	.	.	.	.	.	.	.	.	.	.	.	.	.	1
N2	.	.	.	.20	.	.	.	.	.	.	.	.20	.	.	.	.	.	.	.	.	.	.	.	.	.60
N3	.	.	.	.	.	.	.	.	.	.	.	.	1	.	.	.	.	.	.	.	.	.	.	.	.
N6	.	.	.	.	.	.	.	.	.	.	.	.	.	1	.	.	.	.	.	.	.	.	.	.	.
R1	.	.	.	.	.	1	.	.	.	.	.	.	.	.	.	.	.	.	.	.	.	.	.	.	.
A1	.	.	.	.	.	.	.	.	.	.	.	.	.	.11	.	.	.	.11	.	.	.11	.	.	.	.66
A3	.	.	.	.	.	.	.	.	.	.	.	.	.	.	.	.	.	.	.	.	.	.	.	.	1
A5	.	.	.	.	.	.	.	.	.	.50	.	.	.	.	.	.	.	.	.	.	.	.	.	.	.50
A7	.	.	.	.	.	.	.	.	.	.	.	.	.	.	.	.	.	.	.	.	.	.	.	.	1
A9	.	.	.	.	.	.	.	.	.	.	.	.	.	.	.	.	.	1	.	.	.	.	.	.	.
V28	.	.	.	.	.	.	.	.	.	.	.	.	.	.	.	.	.	.	.	.	.	.	.	.	1
V29	.	.	.	.	.	.	.	.	.	.	.	.	.	.	.	.	.	.	.	.	.	.	.	.	1

AUXI Phase IV Transitional Probabilities

	S3	S4	P1	P4	P5	P7	V3	V4	V14	V16	V17	V18	V21	V22	N1	N2	N3	N4	N5	N6	R1	A1	A5	A9	V28	E
A	.	.	.80	.02	.08	.08	.	.	.	.	.	.	.	.	.	.	.	.	.	.	.	.	.	.	.	.
S3	.	.	.	.	.	.	.	.	.	1	.	.	.	.	.	.	.	.	.	.	.	.	.	.	.	.
S4	.	.	.	.	.	.	.	.	.	.	1	.	.	.	.	.	.	.	.	.	.	.	.	.	.	.
P1	.	.	.	.	.	.	.	.90	.	.	.	.	.04	.	.	.	.04	.	.	.	.	.	.	.	.	.
P4	.	.	1	.	.	.	.	.	.	.	.	.	.	.	.	.	.	.	.	.	.	.	.	.	.	.
P5	.	.	.75	.25	.	.	.	.	.	.	.	.	.	.	.	.	.	.	.	.	.	.	.	.	.	.
P7	.	.	.	.	.	.	.	.75	.	.	.	.	.	.	.	.	.	.	.	.25	.	.	.	.	.	.
V3	.	.	.	.	.	.	.	.	.	.	.	.	.	.	.	.	.	.	.	.	.	.	.	.	.	1
V4	.02	.	.	.	.	.	.02	.	.04	.	.17	.42	.	.19	.	.	.02	.	.	.	.	.	.	.	.02	.08
V14	.	.	.	.	.	.	.	.	.	.	.	.	.	.	.	.	.	.	.	.	.	.	.	.	.	1
V16	.	.	.	.	.	.	.	.	.	.	.	.	.	.	.	.	.	.	.	.	.	.	.	.	.	1
V17	.	.	.	.	.	.	.	.	.	.	.	.36	.	.09	.	.18	.	.	.	.	.	.	.	.	.	.36
V18	.	.03	.	.	.	.	.	.	.	.	.06	.03	.	.	.03	.	.03	.	.	.	.	.13	.06	.17	.	.41
V21	.	.	.	.	.	.	.	1	.	.	.	.	.	.	.	.	.	.	.	.	.	.	.	.	.	.
V22	.	.	.	.	.	.	.	.	.	.	.	.18	.	.	.09	.18	.	.	.	.	.	.09	.	.	.	.45
N1	.	.	.	.	.	.	.	.	.	.	.	.	.	.	.25	.	.25	.	.	.	.	.	.	.	.	.50
N2	.	.	.	.	.	.	.	.	.	.16	.	.16	.	.	.	.	.	.16	.	.	.	.	.	.	.	.50
N3	.	.	.	.	.	.	.	.14	.	.	.	.	.	.	.28	.	.14	.28	.14	.	.	.	.	.	.	.
N4	.	.	.	.	.	.	.	.	.	.	.	.	.	.	.33	.33	.	.	.	.	.	.	.	.	.	.33
N5	.	.	.	.	.	.	.	.	.	.	.	.	.	.	.	.	.	.	.	.	1	.	.	.	.	.
N6	.	.	.	.	.	.	.	1	.	.	.	.	.	.	.	.	.	.	.	.	.	.	.	.	.	.
R1	.	.	.	.	.	.	.	1	.	.	.	.	.	.	.	.	.	.	.	.	.	.	.	.	.	.
A1	.	.	.	.	.	.	.	.	.	.	.	.16	.	.	.16	.16	.	.	.	.	.	.	.	.	.	.50
A5	.	.	.	.	.	.	.	.	.	.	.	.	.	.50	.	.	.	.	.	.	.	.	.	.	.	.50
A9	.	.	.	.	.	.	.	.	.	.	.	.	.	.	.	.	.	.	.	.	.	.20	.	.	.	.80
V28	.	.	.	.	.	.	.	.	.	.	.	.	.	.	.	.	.	.	.	.	.	.	.	.	.	1

4.6 Summary of the Overall Patterns of Structural Change

This summary focuses on the systematic patterns of change in sentence structure over the nine week period of development observed. All sentences types described were present from the onset of the study and the nature of the development process is inferred from the patterns observed and the stage of development exhibited in each case.

The development of sentence structure is marked by a recurrent dominance or high frequency of specific constituent types. Probability values of constituents occurring in predicative position reach a maximum of .80 at the peak of each successive period of dominance.

In the two most frequent sentence types, SV and AUXI, pronouns occur in subject position with a probability of approximately .95 during the greater part of the period of observation. In predicative position these sentence types first exhibit a dominance of objects, which gradually decreases. The decrease in object dominance in SV is accompanied by an increase in the use of adverbs, adverbial phrases and adjectives, and at the same time the occurrence of nouns and nominal phrases in subject position increases markedly in probability from an overall average of .05 to .23 in Phase IV, i.e. the two final weeks of the observation period. Sentences with nouns and nominal phrases in subject position therefore show a dominance of word classes with adverbial and adjectival function. Indications are that the emergence of nouns and nominal phrases in subject position is coupled with a focus on structures with adverbial function in predicative position. This pattern points to a recurrence of successive periods of dominance or focus on different syntactic categories; a period of focus on adverbial phrases may again be followed by that of objects, this time with nouns and nominal phrases in subject position.

The pattern of development observed in sentence types INV and SUB lends support to the assumption that the period of dominance of objects in predicative position is preceded by a dominance of adverbial structures. Here a decrease in the use of adverbial and adjectival phrases is seen to occur. This decrease in probability, however, is accompanied by a gradual increase in the occurrence of objects, a period of focus on adverbial phrases is being replaced by that of object phrases, with pronouns as the dominant word class in subject position. If these observations are correct, INV and SUB are approaching a stage of development at the end of this observation period similar to that exhibited by SV and AUXI at the beginning, i.e. nine weeks earlier. The order of application of these sentence types in production and the stage of development attained in each type may therefore be assessed on the basis of the following criteria:

(i) the probability of occurrence of pronouns versus nouns and nominal phrases in subject position

(ii) the accompanying dominance in predicative position, first of adv./adj. phrases, followed by phrases with object function.

Since SV and AUXI have reached the period of object dominance they precede the remaining types INV and SUB in order of application in production. SV can be placed before AUXI on the basis of the increased occurrence of nouns and noun phrases in subject position. All other sentence types still exhibit a dominance of pronouns in subject position.
The probability of occurrence of structures with object function is higher in INV than in SUB at the end of the period of observation, thus indicating that INV is in advance of SUB in order of application. Furthermore, the occurrence of adverbials in SUB is still on the increase in the early stages of observation, while INV exhibits an overall decrease in these structures.

The order of application of these sentence types in production is therefore postulated as:

SV
AUXI
INV
SUB

The number of sentences with copular verbs is too low to permit a reliable analysis of the pattern of development within this sub-set. Judging by the appearance of nouns in subject position in these sentences, this verb type may precede transitive verbs in order of application. Felix (1977) in a study of child second language acquisition also reports a precedence of this sentence type in order of emergence.

The process of change in the internal structure of simple sentences (SV) can be summarised as follows:

SV		Word Order		
Phase	Constituents:	SUBJ	VEGR	ADVE/ADJE
I	word class:	pronouns	intrans.	simple adverbs, noun phrases
		SUBJ	VEGR	OBJE
II		pronouns	trans.	pronouns/simple nouns, noun phrases
III				ADVE + ADVE
				ADVE + OBJE
IV		SUBJ nouns	VEGR	ADVE/ADJE

The following values show that the categories ADVE and OBJE decrease in complexity over the first three phases:

Transitions (SV)	Predicative position	I	II	III	IV
V1 - N expansions	complex OBJE	.58	.50	.44	.40
V2 - A expansions	complex ADVE	.62	.36	.25	.43

Interestingly, only ADVE shows a definite increase in complexity in Phase IV. This is possibly linked with the new phase of ADVE/ADJE dominance accompanying the appearance of nouns and nominal phrases in subject position. The overall decrease in complexity of these constituents during the first three phases is accompanied by a gradual increase in the number of constituents occurring in these sentences.

Transitions (SV)	Predicative position	I	II	III	IV
V1 V2	ADVE + OBJE	.08	.21	.18	.28
V2 V1	OBJE + ADVE	0	.09	.06	0
V2 V2	ADVE + ADVE*	.25	.19	.25	.12
V1 V1	OBJE + OBJE	.05	0	.04	.04

***ADVE-ADVE describe combinations of adverbials denoting place and time**

These values show that the sequence VEGR ADVE OBJE and VEGR ADVE ADVE is more probable than VEGR OBJE ADVE.

The sentence type <u>AUXI</u> shows a similar pattern of development to SV.

Transitions (AUXI)	Predicative position	I	II	III	IV
V18 - A	complex ADVE	.64	.46	.32	.36
V22 - N	complex OBJE	.44	.38	.29	.27

Here again, both categories continue to decrease in complexity while ADVE shows a slight increase in Phase IV. The following values indicate the overall increase in the number of constituents occurring in the sentence.

Transitions	Predicative position	I	II	III	IV
V17 V18	OBJE (pronoun) + ADVE	.28	.22	.30	.36
V22 V18	OBJE (noun) + ADVE	.07	.20	.23	.18
V18 V18	ADVE + ADVE	.07	.04	.15	.03
V18 V17	ADVE + OBJE (pronoun)	.03	0	.03	.06
V18 V22	ADVE + OBJE (noun)	.03	.09	.11	0

As in SV, OBJE ADVE VEGR shows an increase in probability of occurrence and the sequence OBJE ADVE VEGR is more likely to occur than ADVE OBJE VEGR.

In summary, the categories ADVE and OBJE first appear individually in these sentences and show a gradual increase in complexity. Their subsequent simplification is accompanied by an increase in the occurrence of both categories within one sentence. The pattern of development of complex structures observed in INV and SUB is not as clear cut due to the low frequency of occurrence of these sentence types compared to SV and AUXI. The probabilities observed on phrase level are subject to the fluctuations typical of small samples. A certain trend in development is nevertheless discernible.

Transitions (INV)		I	II	III	IV
V15 - A	complex ADVE	.23	.16	.08	.04
(V15 - N)	complex OBJE	(.30	.21	.28	.11)

Here adverbials show a continuous decrease in complexity. The N-value fluctuations are attributable to their very low frequency of occurrence so that it cannot be stated with certainty whether they are actually decreasing or not.

INV differs from SV and AUXI in that there is no increase in the co-occurrence of ADVE and OBJE in one sentence. This indicates that co-occurrence is a feature of development which occurs when learners have learnt to apply both categories individually, i.e. after the phases of ADVE and OBJE dominance.

Transitions (INV)	Predicative position	I	II	III	IV
V1 V2	OBJE + ADVE	0	0	.11	.08
V2 V2	ADVE + ADVE	.20	.33	0	0
V2 V1	ADVE + OBJE	.20	0	.50	.20

The pattern of development within SUB clearly reflects its less advanced stage of development, here the dominant category ADVE is still increasing in complexity over the first three phases and does not show any decrease until phase IV.

Transitions (SUB)		I	II	III	IV
V10 - AV	complex ADVE	.27	.49	.66	.52
(V13 - N)	complex OBJE	(.16	0	.27	.08)

As the following table shows the categories ADVE and OBJE do not co-occur systematically, their frequency of occurrence in absolute terms being very low.

Transitions		I	II	III	IV
V10 V10	ADVE + ADVE	(.18	0	0	0)
V10 V13	ADVE + OBJE	(0	.08	0	0)
V13 V10	OBJE + ADVE	(0	.16	.27	.16)

Thus, the pattern of increase and decrease in complexity lends further support to the order of development of these sentence types set out above. One final remark on the patterns observed relates to the sequence of integration of both categories ADVE and OBJE: In all cases ADVE is adjoined to VEGR, i.e. to the element it modifies. In SV the pattern is SVAO and not SVOA, in SUB and AUXI, where the verb appears at the end of the clause, SOAV is a more probable sequence than SAOV (cf. higher probability of sequence OBJE + ADVE above under SUB).

SV		I	II	III	IV
V1 V2	VEGR ADVE OBJE	.08	.21	.25	.28
V2 V1	VEGR OBJE ADVE	0	.09	.06	0

AUXI					
V18 V17	ADVE OBJE VEGR	.03	0	.03	.06
V18 V22		.03	.09	.11	0
V17 V18	OBJE ADVE VEGR	.28	.22	.30	.36
V22 V18		.07	.20	.23	.18

Example of VEGR ADVE OBJE:

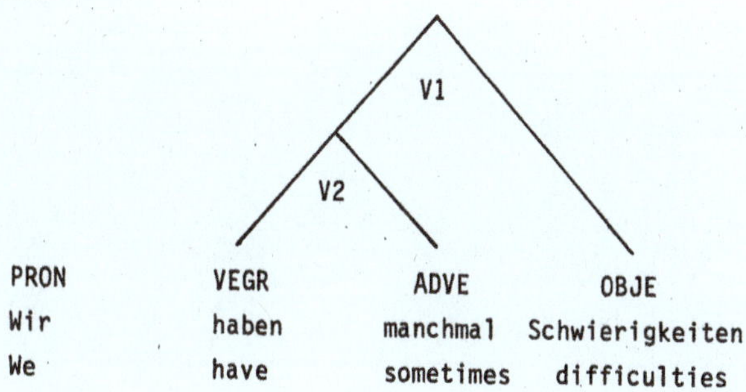

Interestingly, the pattern of development of the most advanced learner of the group, Karin, whose data were separated from the others, shows a trend towards a dominance of SVOA sequences. If this is not coincidental it would mean that patterns of dominance already observed also occur at this level of development; SVAO precedes SVOA.

As shown above, subordinate clauses with adverbial function appear systematically before those with object function.
By virtue of the dominance of OBJE in the two most frequent sentence types SV and AUXI, infinitives are more likely to occur as objects or as object complements. Infinitives with adverbial function are comparatively infrequent, while infinitives with subject function are confined to copular sentences. Relative clauses appear mainly in predicative position (object modification); instances of subject modification are very low. However, the frequency of infinitives, relative clauses and wh-clauses is too low to permit a precise analysis of their order and context of emergence.

In summary, the results of the data analysis show that the pattern of development in speech production can be characterised as involving recurrent periods of focus on specific syntactic relations. These are marked by patterns of dominance of syntactic categories in various positions in the sentence types analysed.

5. SIMILARITIES WITH PATTERNS OF DEVELOPMENT REPORTED IN OTHER STUDIES

The pattern of development presented above compares in some important respects with those reported in longitudinal studies on the acquisition of German as a second language by children in naturalistic settings. "Repetitive orders" of development were first reported by Felix (1977) in child second language development. The children, whose mother tongue was English, were aged between four and seven years. They received no formal instruction in the language and since they were living with their English-speaking families, communication in German was mainly confined to contacts with neighbourhood friends. The data is based on conversational recordings (adult-child) which took place two to three times per week for a period of eight to ten months.

At levels of development comparable to those reached by the group of learners presented above, Felix reports the following findings: "The subject of the first copular sentences to appear is invariably the demonstrative pronoun 'das'". These sentences show a predominance of nouns in predicate position; adjectives appear later, followed by prepositional phrases.[7] With the introduction of the personal pronoun "ich" in subject position, "we encounter the same order of acquisition in the area of categories in predicate position".

These results show that with respect to the phenomenon of recurrent orders, close similarities exist between the pattern found in child and adult second language acquisition of German.

In a longitudinal study of the acquisition of German by three Italian-speaking children (aged approx. 8 years) from immigrant worker families, Pienemann (1980, 1981) found orders of development which are again in some respects similar to those set out above. A full comparison cannot be made, however, since the order of acquisition is classified in terms of underlying structures which the learner is presumed to be in possession of but deletes at the surface structure level on account of limitations in processing capacity. A sequence such as "ein madchen bier" (a girl beer), for example, is assigned the structure NP V NP although no verb is actually produced.

---

[7] A reliable comparison of the order of emergence of word classes within sentences with a copula cannot be made on account of their relatively low frequency of occurrence in the present data base.

The order of development reported is as follows:

NP + V
NP + V + PP*
NP + V + NP
NP + Kop + NP
NP + V + PP + PP
NP + V + NP + PP

As in the data of English-speaking students acquiring German, adverbials appear in predicate position before objects, and "the extension of a sentence always starts with an adverbial" (1980, 35). Other similarities refer to the order of acquisition of sentence types - sentences with an auxiliary or modal verb which require separation of the infinitive or participle as in "wir sind nach Hause gegangen" (we have home gone) (i.e. AUXI) are mastered before sentences requiring subject verb inversion (INV). Furthermore, inversion does not occur at all after complex adverbials in sentence initial position. As Pienemann points out the pattern of development consists of a successive cancellation of "restrictions in applicational contexts" of structures.

However, it is assumed that second language learners rely on prior syntactic knowledge from the outset in organising their second language. The fact that there is no evidence in the learner's output of syntactic structuring during the phase of one and two word utterances is attributed to memory and processing constraints: lexical search procedures, for instance, are thought to prevent application of syntactic knowledge (cf. Pienemann, 1981, 79).

The type of syntactic organisation is presumed to involve a NVN ordering of elements and is based on Bever (1970) who postulated the following strategy: any noun-verb-noun (NVN) sequence with a potential internal unit in the surface structure corresponds to 'actor-action-object' (1970, 298). Bever's own observations, however, show that children at the age of approximately 3;6 are less inclined, in comprehension tests, to interpret NVN sequences as an agent-action-object relation than older children. Similar observations were made by Maratsos (1974); younger children make less errors in interpreting passive sentences than slightly older children, and performance

*PP = prepositional phrase.

disimproves before finally being mastered. In a comprehension study conducted by Sinclair and Bronckart (1972) with children learning French, evidence is presented which indicates that sensitivity to word order is not characteristic of the earlier stages of development. Such processing strategies were not clearly established before the age of five in that particular group.

In a recent cross-linguistic re-investigation of the status of this strategy and children's sensitivity to word order as a means of processing language Slobin and Bever (1982) report (again on the basis of comprehension tests) that children learn what is referred to as the 'canonical'[8] sentence form of their particular language. In the word-order based languages investigated, i.e. Italian and English, this is NVN (SVO). In Turkish, where structural relations are marked inflectionally, the canonical order is NNV (SOV). While Turkish children master the inflectionally based 'canonical' form from the earliest stages, English and Italian children do not exhibit sensitivity to word order as a means of processing language input until the stage of 3 phrase utterances (which average approximately five words) is reached. Sensitivity to word order is little better than chance prior to then.

As Slobin and Bever point out, the conclusion which these observations allow is that the syntactic organisation which emerges is the result of an 'inductive capacity' which allows learners to identify and compare the various surface structure forms in the language they are learning and not of the application of any 'fundamental' processing strategy. It is an empirical question whether second language learners also apply inductive analyses before establishing a predominant processing schema for the language they are learning.

As numerous studies of pidgin systems have demonstrated the existence of prior syntactic knowledge, for example, provides no guarantee that learners will always resort to it in organising their second language. Furthermore, by postulating a high level of underlying competence from the outset it may be impossible to recognise changes in the status of elements during acquisition; the status of a structure at one level may be fundamentally different from that which it acquires through re-organisation of the system at later

[8] The canonical form is not the most frequent but that which is most neutral with respect to 'discourse presuppositions'. These are sentences which "most clearly reveal basic schema of syntactic organisation"(cf.Slobin,Bever, 1982).

stages.
Pienemann emphasises the necessity of taking such factors as processing capacity and perceptual strategies into account in studying the processes involved in language development. Although the focus of interest is mainly structural,detailed descriptions are given where learners produce or fail to produce certain structures.

In the present study, variations in performance are not treated as 'deletions', as a 'failure' to produce unterlying structures. The view held here is that orders of application in production follow a systematic pattern, "deletions" follow a specific principle and, secondly, correspondence between orders of application in language production and the principles whereby syntactic knowledge is organised in the underlying system may be less than hitherto presumed. Order of appearance or mastery in production may be only indirectly linked with orders of organisation in the underlying system.

Some evidence of similar patterns of development can also be found in the data of adult immigrant workers. In a study of the acquisition of German by Italian and Spanish immigrant workers comparable patterns are reported at advanced stages of development. "The acquisition of subordinate clauses shows a very clear distinct order: adverbial clauses are learned before nominal clauses, nominal clauses before relative clauses". (Klein, Dittmar, 1979).
These comparisons suffice to demonstrate that similarities in patterns of development can be found across differing learning situations, both with and without intensive formal tuition. For the group of learners studied here frequency of attendance at language class did not in principle affect the pattern observed.[9]
This observation has led some researchers (Krashen most notably) to posit two basically different modes of language development: one by way of "acquisition" where learners draw on innate endowments in acquiring a language. This process is assumed to be inherently systematic, mainly unconscious and therefore distinct from language "learning" which involves <u>conscious</u>

[9]The one learner, Joe, who dropped out of the language class entirely, did not exhibit any fundamental difference in rate or course of development over the nine weeks observed.

assimilation of knowledge of the language. A discussion of this distinction, which forms the basis of what is known as the "Monitor Theory" will be given at the end of the next section.

5.1 Transitional Stages

The results presented above show that changes in the underlying grammar are gradual and not discrete. Structures which are in the process of being replaced exist side by side with their replacements; rule addition does not immediately incur equivalent rule loss.
The extent to which the order of re-organisation in the underlying system is directly reflected in the patterns of application in production remains unclear, however. One-to-one correspondence is unlikely since orders of development in production reflect the influence of factors inherent to conditions applying during the encoding process in ongoing communication. These factors will be discussed in detail in the next section.

Studies in language acquisition start from the assumption that the observation of how learners use language during the process of development will shed light on the principles whereby this knowledge is acquired. In these endeavours the focus of interest has been primarily structuralist. Within this framework variation in the application of knowledge is generally treated as the imperfect functioning of a presumed underlying structure or ability.

Through the systematic inclusion in analyses of parameters such as variation in behaviour in real time, in its social context etc., it can be shown that consistencies in behaviour are related to what have been termed performance factors, and not only to specific underlying structures such as the language learner's knowledge base or competence. A clear understanding of these factors and their influence on patterns of development in language production is required before assumptions can be made about the less observable 'structural' level. The following section is devoted to a discussion of one of these factors.

6. LEARNING WHILE PERFORMING: BEHAVIOUR ORGANISATION IN LANGUAGE PRODUCTION

As the probabilities of occurrence show, learners do not draw on all available structures with equal likelihood but focus on various sub-sets of the system putting each one into practice in turn during the learning process.

A period of focus is marked by an increase in the probability of occurrence of a particular structure which extends over a certain period. This feature of the learning process in language production is most pronounced in the elaboration of sentence structure where constituents are systematically applied in turn in predicate position. Marked increases in probability of occurrence are later followed by a comparable decrease when attention is shifted to the next constituent type in order of application.

The set order of application is repeated in each sentence type in succession. Simple sentences (SV) are first constructed with a predominance of pronouns in subject position, predicate relations are first restricted to occurrences of adverbs, adverbial phrases and adjectives. This predominance of adverbials and adjectives is replaced by a period of focus on object relations. A shift in focus to sentence initial position occurs only when this cycle of learning has been completed in predicate position. The predominance of pronouns in subject position is slowly replaced by an increase in the use of simple nouns. Indications are that the same cycle of learning is repeated with nouns in subject position - predicate relations are again first restricted to occurrences of adverbials and adjectives.[10]

Each sentence type follows the set pattern of learning regardless of the overall stage of elaboration reached in other sub-sets. Subordinate clauses emerge at a point when the two most frequent sentence types SV and AUXI (cf. p. 49) have progressed to the period of focus on objects. The stage

---

[10] The full cycle could not be documented as the period of observation ended here. Tentative evidence is nevertheless observable in various sentence types.

of development reached here is not automatically transferred to embedded clauses, which begin with a dominance of adverbials before proceeding to a period of focus on object relations.
As mentioned above, with the systematic emergence of nouns and noun phrases in subject position in simple sentences predicate relations are again restricted to the occurrence of simple adverbials and adjectives, although learners were capable of producing all phrase types in this context with pronouns in subject position. The set cycle of learning applies across all sentence types in turn, with no transfer of learning from one context to the next.

Although these learners can be said to have acquired a range of grammatical relations, their applicability is subject to constraints which can hardly be ascribed to a lack of knowledge of such relations. These constraints are coupled with a focussing principle which also shows that what appears in production cannot be taken as a simple reflection of the extent of organisation of the underlying system. The consistent application of any structure over an extensive period does not result from a lack of other options. If the principles underlying these features of the learning process are not structurally based, the order of application need not necessarily be structurally motivated either. Here, two further aspects of the learning process are noteworthy: on the word class level there is some evidence of a progression from simple to complex. The first adverbials to appear are simple adverbs like "here" and "there", simple nouns and complex nominal groups later. The first objects are pronouns and simple nouns, with complex nominals following later. The occurrence of subject verb inversion in sentences with adverbials in initial position as in

'dann fahre ich nach Hause'

'then go I home'

is dependent on the complexity of the sentence constituents (cf. p. 68); if the adverbial preceding or following the verb is complex, i.e. a nominal group such as 'the following Monday' learners will apply the SV sequence with which they are more familiar and not the inversion. Therefore, the application of a rule of grammar at a particular point in development is seen to depend, among other factors, on the complexity of the constituents, or the other rules with which it co-occurs, as well as the extent to which these have previously been put into practice.

It has generally been assumed that the essential facts of language development can be accounted for by specifying the rules describing the knowledge acquired. As the results described above show, the application of knowledge during learning is obviously subject to additional factors. In his study of the acquisition of inflectional morphemes in first language development, Brown (1973) comments on the characteristics of the observed acquisition order as follows: "There is always a considerable period, varying in length with the particular morpheme, in which production where required is probabilistic. This is a fact which does not accord well with the notion that the acquisition of grammar is a matter of the acquisition of rules, since rules in the generative grammar either apply or do not apply. One would expect rule acquisition to be sudden." (p. 285) In child second language development 'repetitive orders' similar to those described above were first reported by Felix (1977, see above). According to Felix "The child does not acquire the structure or structural feature involved once and for all at a given stage in development, but will have to re-acquire - under certain conditions and in roughly the same order - subsets of structures which had already occurred previously in a different environment."
The subject of the first copula sentences to appear is invariably the demonstrative pronoun "das". These sentences contain only nouns in predicate position; adjectives appear later followed by prepositional phrases. With the introduction of the personal pronoun "ich" (I) in subject position "we encounter the same order of acquisition in the area of categories in predicate position." Felix takes the view that predicate relations already present in the system have to be re-acquired with the appearance of each new element, and that this pattern reflects the actual process of acquisition.

The view taken here is that orders of development in language production need not directly reflect the process of acquisition in terms of the underlying system. The separation of these two levels is motivated by the nature of the restrictions described above: at any point in the learning process the overall stage of elaboration can be shown to be more advanced in those sub-sets of the system which appear first in production. These are simple SV-structures with pronouns in subject position, the copula as verb, and an adverb, adjective or adverbial phrase in predicate position. This first phase is followed by a period in which transitive verbs appear with increasingly complex object relations. With the subsequent introduction of nouns in subject position constituents appearing in predicative position are again restricted to adverbs, adjectives and adverbial phrases. New structures are applied in production in this sequence, always beginning with those contexts which have been longest in practice, followed by the next, and so on.

With 'complexity' defined as the order of emergence we see that probability of occurrence is determined by the cumulative complexity of all the constituents in a particular sentence. Whether subject verb inversion will occur in sentences with an adverbial phrase in sentence initial position or not depends on the type of verb (copula or otherwise) whether the subject is a pronoun, noun or nominal phrase, the complexity of the adverbial phrase in initial position and the type and complexity of the other constituents. A 'simple' verb such as the copula occurring in conjunction with complex constituents may be equal in complexity to a more 'complex' verb (transitives) occurring with structurally simple constituents. Occurrence of SV inversion may be equally probable in both contexts, but may not yet be occurring where transitive verbs appear with structurally complex nominal phrases.

In summary, constraints on the application of a grammatical structure in production cannot be readily attributed to a lack of knowledge as such. Complexity, which refers here not only to structural features but also to order of emergence in production, constitutes a central constraint. The application of a structure in each context is also marked by a steady increase in probability of occurrence which holds over a certain period until focus of attention is shifted to another new structure. This pattern of behaviour with its obvious connotations of 'pattern drills' indicates that what is selected for production does not directly depend on presence in the underlying system.

A further characteristic of learner behaviour in production would seem to be relevant in this context. Variation in learner performance is a widely reported phenomenon in the literature on language learning and acquisition. 'Focus on form' rather than content leads to variations in output[11] not only

[11] cf., for instance, Krashen (1981)

with learners receiving formal tuition but has also been reported where the influence of formal tuition can be ruled out. An example of this type of variation is reported by Labov & Labov (1977) in a study of their daughter's acquisition of WH-questions in first language development. At a certain stage of development inversion of the subject verb sequence occurred after all WH-words except 'why' even though the child "did know about and could imitate the adult rule" (p. 9). However, in a question game involving the use of 'why' the child's overall performance showed a much higher success rate 22/26 (84%) after 'why' than in everyday conversational exchanges where the application rate for the inversion rule amounted to only 4%(13/292).

Focus on form, which amounts to an increase in attentional or processing capacity on this level, leads to an increase in the production of more 'advanced forms' compared to the level observed in day-to-day conversational exchanges where the focus is generally on the communicative aspect of the task. This demonstrates that the learner's output does not always stand in a one-to-one relation with his or her overall knowledge. The pattern of development with accompanying 'learning focus' described above, i.e. patterned increases and decreases in probability of occurrence, is interpreted here as a principle of behaviour organisation which facilitates learning under conditions where attentional capacity is limited - as is the case in language production. The learner does not put all aspects of the acquired system into practice simultaneously but selects and focuses on different subsets in succession. This selectivity allows the learner to deal with the problem of learning a task while having to perform it.

As pointed out by J.B. Carroll (1971) and Levelt (1975) the specification of acquired knowledge alone cannot adequately account for the learner's behaviour during learning, "what is required are additional principles of learning and behaviour organisation. Such a theory has not been developed in the framework of cognitive code learning" (Levelt, 1975, p. 53). In language production a number of operations have to be carried out in an appropriate temporal sequence, successful accomplishment requires that sufficient attentional capacity be available for each aspect of the task. The encoding process is generally thought of as being guided by a hierarchical system of plans or routines. One of the central aspects of skill in performance is that the creation of plans during the encoding process is reduced to a minimum. The result of automation is that less and less effort is required for lower-level activity leaving more attentional capacity for higher level decisions (cf. Levelt, 1975; Kahneman 1973; Miller et al., 1960).

Selectional constraints along with the focussing principle facilitate automation-through-repetition in language production so that the orders of application may be more aptly described as 'orders of automation' rather than 'orders of acquisition'. It remains to be clarified in what way these relate to the actual order of construction of the underlying grammar. If these observations hold, factors governing the pattern of development in production are not solely structural in nature.

These observations are largely based on stretches of performance which were selected according to the criterion 'ease of production'.[12] These involved thematically.coherent groups of utterances which evidenced relatively low occurrences of hesitational phenomena as well as little overt attention to form. These were passages in which learners encountered no major difficulties in expressing what they wished to convey. It goes without saying that learners do have such difficulties and an analysis of such passages whould yield different probabilities of occurrence to those set out above.
As discussed above, variations in attentional capacity which result in an increase in the amount of attention available on one level, as when the learner is in a position to focus on form, lead to changes in the selectional constraints on the application of rules. If the hypothesis holds that these selectional constraints reflect a routine or learning procedure designed to facilitate learning in an ongoing process, its implementation or suspension must be guided by a higher level organisational system which controls application of the various options holding during the encoding process. The organisational or control system must therefore have access to information from various sources during the encoding process. In sentence generation information must be accessible on the options available for encoding a specific message so that items can be selected and assessments made as to the mutual constraints involved. The options will be defined by the learner's knowledge of the language, the phase of development reached by the learning procedure, along with the momentary attentional capacity of the learner. Assessments can be expected to start from some 'given' which may be defined by the phase

[12] This criterion was set in order to increase comparability between learners on the performance level.

of development reached by the learning procedure. If, for instance, a learner has proceeded in one particular context from a period of application of predicate relations to expanding the subject category, then this latter point may in that phase constitute the set priority from which other specific constraints follow, given a certain attentional span etc. If the subject of a sentence at a certain stage of development should consist of a noun or nominal group this fact entails specific constraints on the applicability of the predicate relations already at the learner's disposal, given 'average' performance conditions. Since these constraints can apparently be suspended by an increase in attentional capacity this means that the learning procedure does not apply rigidly but is subordinate to a higher order organisational level which monitors the interaction of various systems during the encoding process and operates in terms of selectional procedures which can be characterised as "if x then y".

As yet, little can be said about the principles on which these procedures are based, why some structural relations require less attentional capacity than others and are therefore recurrently easier to perform, and what these relations convey about the organisation of the underlying system or the way in which it is constructed. It is questionable whether those relations which are first applied on sentence level in production are those which are first organised in the underlying system. They may be the simplest of a certain category but not necessarily the first. The pattern of development in production described above shows that a one-to-one correspondence between these levels is unlikely, that learning in language production is basically characterised by recurrent phases of "automation-through-repetition" and that these may be only indirectly related to actual orders of acquisition. In the formal grammar defined above the 'control language' which reflects the constraints on the application of rules (or to be more precise, on pairs of rules in derivations) forms an integral part of the grammar. The constraints, however, are only partially syntactical in nature[13] and are for the most part determined by organisational principles in language production,and a language procedure which is designed to facilitate the learning process while encoding messages in real time. The probability of application of one rule of grammar over another is a factor which is not solely dependent on grammatical knowledge and in psycholinguistic terms grammars need not be defined so as to predict behaviour during learning when this is determined by factors which are of an extrinsic nature.

[13] Some combinatorial possibilities are also excluded by virtue of the way in which the rules are defined.

Theoretical developments in the study of language have long depended on a distinction between questions of 'performance' and questions of 'competence'. This distinction implies that a description of language is logically distinct from an account of the way users implement their knowledge during speech performance. In one respect this is correct; there is at least no simple one-to-one correspondence between these levels during learning. However, the problem with this distinction lies not in the fact that it has been drawn, but in the fact that it has led to the total isolation of these levels. 'Performance' has in the process been equated with error variance. Within the competence/performance distinction, competence is taken as the exclusive domain of systematic behaviour. Systematic features of language behaviour have thereby been all too readily, as well as erroneoulsy, attributed to the competence level in language learning.
Language learning is a complex skill in which a number of knowledge systems and motor skills are gradually integrated during the learning process. Any attempt to explain the learner's performance in terms of a set of rules deriving from only one aspect of his behaviour fails to capture the complex nature of language learning as a skilled performance and how various levels systematically interact and shape each other.

Increased attention has recently been directed toward the question of the way in which 'performance factors', i.e. encoding and decoding processes, shape the form language takes (cf. Longuet-Higgins 1981, Fodor 1981). Fodor, for instance, argues that restrictions on the application of certain rules have no formal foundation but may be determined by the necessity of reducing ambiguities which arise from the way in which sentences are generally parsed.

A basic issue in first language acquisition concerns the nature of sentence complexity and the terms in which this can be defined. In a study conducted with Japanese children, Hakuta (1980) reports that complexity defined in terms of the linear sequence of constituents in the surface structure and not complexity as defined by grammatical relations constitutes the critical factor in both sentence comprehension and production during language development. Language behaviour is not determined solely by linguistic factors and the role of other cognitive processes in shaping this ability have to be adequately accounted for in any attempt to construct a theory of how language is acquired.

6.1 The "Monitor Theory" and Learning Routines in Language Production

According to the Monitor Theory learners can draw on two fundamentally different knowledge bases when using language. Language can be produced by applying one's knowledge of an acquired system which evolves by way of innate endowments for language learning. This process of 'acquisition' is thought to be inherently systematic, mainly unconscious and therefore distinct from language "learning" which involves conscious assimilation of knowledge of the language, which is then explicitly available to the learner. The role of this latter body of knowledge in language development is said to be largely restricted, it can only be brought into play in modifying the output of the "acquired" system. Utterances cannot be initiated by way of "learned" knowledge. The distinction between acquisition and learning is based on the observation of "natural orders" in the acquisition of the morphemes of English. This order is largely independent of such factors as the order of presentation of items in language class, the learner's source language etc. The acquisition/learning distinction hinges on the observation that when learners have no opportunity of monitoring their output, of checking it and correcting errors, the "difficulty order" in the acquisition of morphemes is "natural", i.e. the kinds of mistakes made with the class of morphemes in question follow a common pattern. When learners are given the opportunity of monitoring their language output, as in the discrete-point testing of grammatical items, the errors found exhibit no common pattern; they are no longer "natural". In the Monitor Theory the "natural order" found under conditions which do not allow for monitoring is taken as evidence of the existence of an "acquired" system working without conscious grammatical knowledge. Deviations from this order are attributed to conscious knowledge, brought into play by the use of the "Monitor".[14]

> "The study of grammatical morphemes has been particularly fruitful for understanding the mechanisms involved in second language acquisition by adults. Aside from telling us in what order certain structures are in fact acquired, these studies have also been of value in revealing the domain of the acquired and learned grammars, when performers appeal to conscious learning and when they do not" (Krashen, 1981, p. 51).

---

[14] For an overview of this theory of the range of conclusions drawn from it cf. Krashen 1981.

The postulation of "natural" and unconscious "acquisition" versus conscious "learning" serves to explain divergent patterns in the language performance of learners during language production under varying conditions. In one case the learners are engaged in communication where, on the whole, little attentional capacity is devoted to formal correctness. The main focus of attention is usually directed toward content. As discussed above, the encoding process is guided by an organisational system which allows for the problem of divided attention during production. The attentional capacity is divided appropriately between the different tasks involved, access to the structures available in the underlying system is restricted or extended according to attentional span. In the type of performance conditions in which the data of the present study were collected, the restrictions holding are observable as systematic orders of application in production. The suspension of the conditions calling for this form of behaviour organisation will lead to the suspension of these orders. With increased attentional capacity on the formal level, as occurs in test situations, learners will also have increased access to other forms present in the underlying system, and not just to those being currently mastered in production.[15] The observation relating to orders of application or automation are all the more relevant here since the morpheme studies do not relate strictly to presence or absence of forms in the learner language but to sequences of overall mastery. A study of self-corrections of morphological errors made in conversation by English and Japanese speaking students acquiring German showed that corrections at this level are similarly guided by principles of behaviour organisation. Learners also focus on different sub-sets of the system in turn, a similar shift in focus across constituent and sentence types was observed (cf. Carroll, 1983).

---

[15]The performance of Labov's daughter is a case in point (see above). Here the improvement in performance observed cannot be readily attributed to monitoring which relys solely on explicit knowledge of rules of grammar. A study by Ninio and Bruner (1978) in first langauge development also supports the observation of the importance of familiarity and processing capacity in language behaviour. New items of language are first observed in interactional settings which are well established and are often restricted to these for some time before being extended to others. Slobin (1981) also reports similar restrictions. Although children are capable of expressing a wide range of conceptual relations at the stage of two- and three-word utterances, the notions which are first marked grammatically are those which are "in some sense salient to the child".(185).

If the hypothesis holds that orders of emergence as well as orders of subsequent mastery in production reflect principles of behaviour organisation inherent in the encoding process, these observations present an alternative explanation of varying patterns of behaviour in learners' productions, thereby calling the basis of the "learning" versus "acquisition" distinction into question.
The role of processing limitations in language learning and the necessity of taking differences between "controlled" versus "automatic" processing into account in its description was raised by McLaughlin (1978) in his criticism of the Monitor Theory. The terms "controlled" versus "automatic" are those used by Schneider and Schiffrin (1977). Here "controlled" processing, which can be either conscious or unconscious, refers to the stage of learning which precedes "automatic" processing. McLaughlin's proposition that "controlled" versus "automatic" presents a more viable distinction than the "conscious" versus "unconscious" knowledge bases of the Monitor Theory in that it can be more readily related to observable data is borne out by the results of the present study. These show evidence of repetitive orders of application, which lead to "mastery" or "automatic" processing in language production. Operations which have not yet been routinised are not accessible unless increased attentional capacity is available.

Variation in the language performance of second language learners and the role of attention has been discussed in detail in Tarone (1982). Here the learner's 'interlanguage' is viewed as consisting of a set of different norms. Attention to speech causes the learner to shift from a 'vernacular' to a 'superordinate' style. The latter is considered more 'permeable to invasion' from other rule systems, such as the target or source language norms. The 'vernacular' is thought to be more internally consistent than the 'superordinate' style. As discussed above the consistency observable in the language learner's system more readily reflects the processes whereby knowledge is implemented and automated in production rather than the way in which knowledge is organised in the underlying system.

As long as the language system is evolving, acquisition will involve the continuous re-organisation (or loss and replacement) of structures that have been fully automated either the last time round or at some previous stage. One could imagine that the longer a particular stage of development is automated the more difficult it will become to implement new structures present in the underlying system. The disadvantages associated with too much practise at any level are more likely to occur in second than in first language learning as a result of inadequate exposure, modest learning ambitions etc. The amount of routinisation experienced in any one phase of development may constitute one of the factors contributing to attainment or non-attainment of target-like ability. The longer a particular phase is automated the more difficult it may become to "shake the habit". It may then be more appropriate in this context of relative system stability to speak of 'vernacular' and 'superordinate' styles as opposed to when systems are in a constant state of flux.

The conclusions which may be drawn from the above results and hypotheses raise more questions than answers with respect to the way in which learners <u>develop</u> their knowledge of a language, as opposed to <u>learning</u> to put this into practice. Orders of application in production may be only indirectly related to the order in which structures are actually acquired and reorganised. More information is required on the principles underlying such selectional constraints in production as well as on the status of the postulated organisational system and the type of information it draws on.[17]

With respect to their didactical implications the above hypotheses do indicate that the role of formal tuition in language development may be less restricted than hitherto postulated within the framework of the Monitor Theory since the orders of application no longer serve as evidence of a separate 'acquired' system and the rigid separation of knowledge bases following from the 'acquired' versus 'learned' distinction need not hold. Restrictions on the assimilation of knowledge cannot be assessed simply on the basis of orders of application in production, nor can these serve as appropriate models for progression in teaching curricula. A theory of language development which attempts to explain how development proceeds in varying contexts will necessarily involve an interaction of theories from different areas. The description of courses of development in terms of only one aspect of the

[17] Given structural options for marking "time at which an action takes place" does this system select among the options available (say adverbial means versus tense markings) on a structural basis such as "include <u>tense markings</u> on <u>verb type</u> x" or are decisions less structural and more along the lines of "attention-span allows for the 'newest' feature, which would involve keeping a record of the order of appearance or organisation of items in the underlying system.

entire process fails to capture the nature of language as a skilled performance and how various aspects of this behaviour interact and shape each other.

APPENDIX

Example 1:

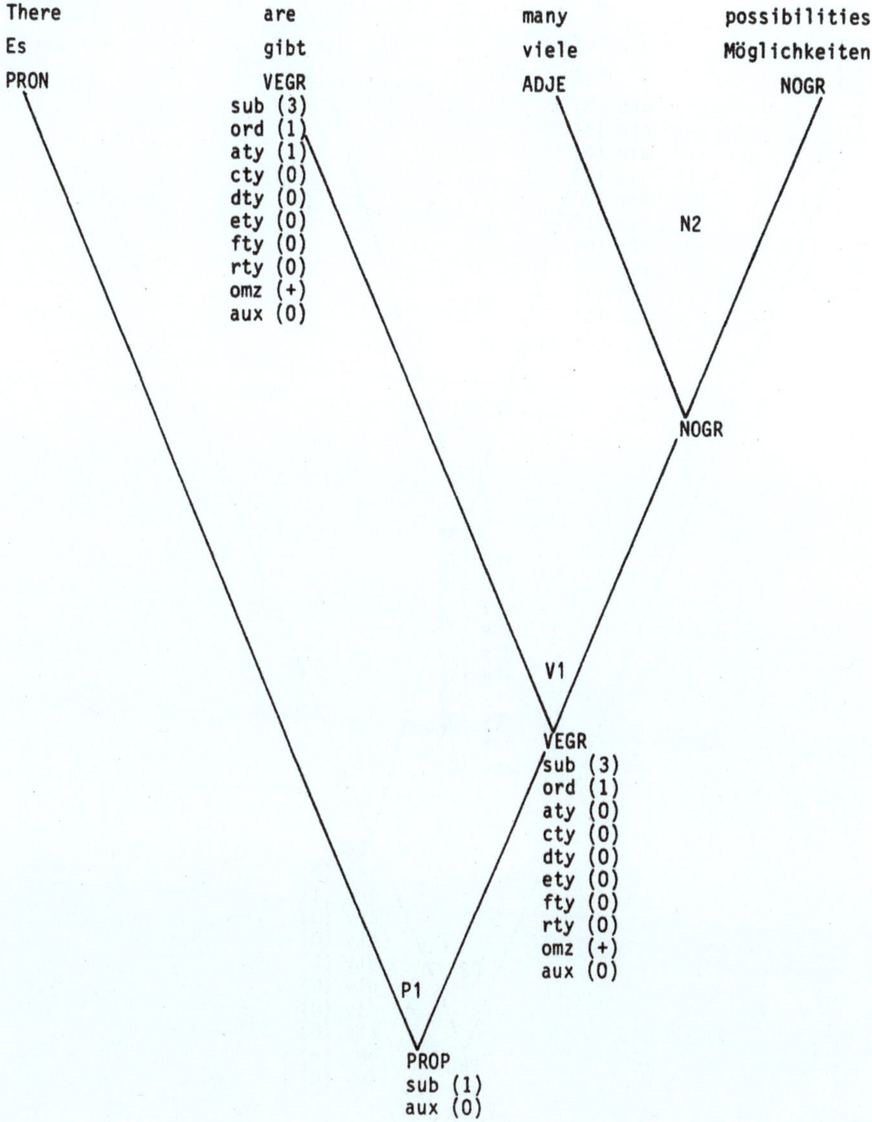

Example 2:

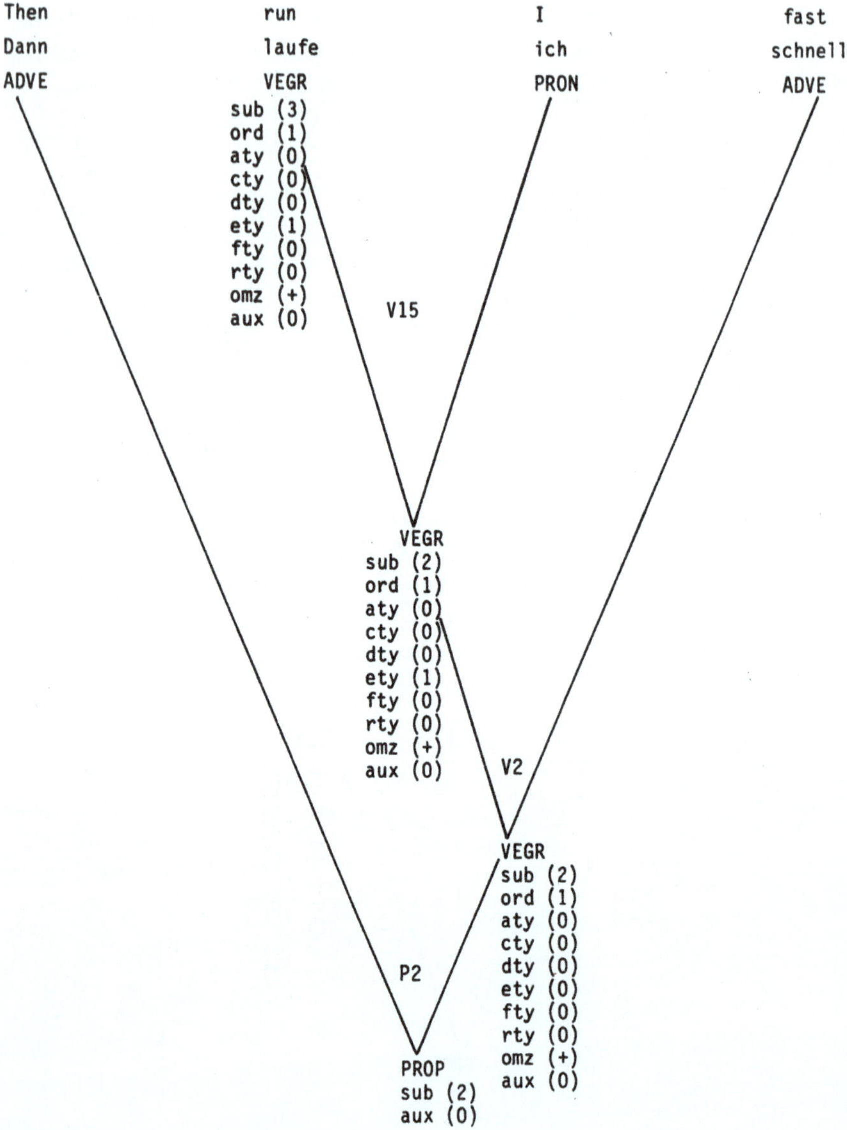
Then
Dann
ADVE
run
laufe
VEGR
sub (3)
ord (1)
aty (0)
cty (0)
dty (0)
ety (1)
fty (0)
rty (0)
omz (+)
aux (0)
I
ich
PRON
fast
schnell
ADVE
V15
VEGR
sub (2)
ord (1)
aty (0)
cty (0)
dty (0)
ety (1)
fty (0)
rty (0)
omz (+)
aux (0)
V2
VEGR
sub (2)
ord (1)
aty (0)
cty (0)
dty (0)
ety (0)
fty (0)
rty (0)
omz (+)
aux (0)
P2
PROP
sub (2)
aux (0)

Example 3:

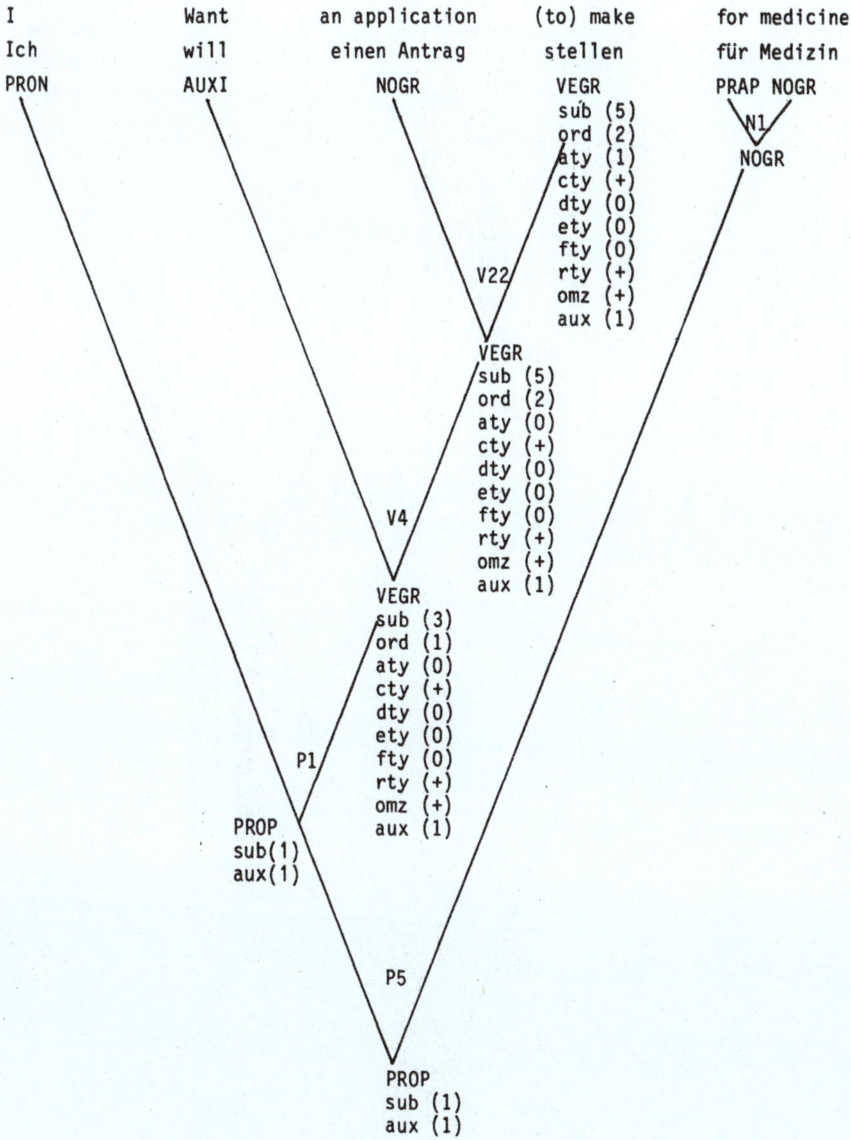
I
Want
an application
(to) make
for medicine
Ich
will
einen Antrag
stellen
für Medizin
PRON
AUXI
NOGR
VEGR
PRAP NOGR
sub (5)
ord (2)
aty (1)
cty (+)
dty (0)
ety (0)
fty (0)
rty (+)
omz (+)
aux (1)
N1
NOGR
V22
VEGR
sub (5)
ord (2)
aty (0)
cty (+)
dty (0)
ety (0)
fty (0)
rty (+)
omz (+)
aux (1)
V4
VEGR
sub (3)
ord (1)
aty (0)
cty (+)
dty (0)
ety (0)
fty (0)
rty (+)
omz (+)
aux (1)
P1
PROP
sub(1)
aux(1)
P5
PROP
sub (1)
aux (1)

Example 4:

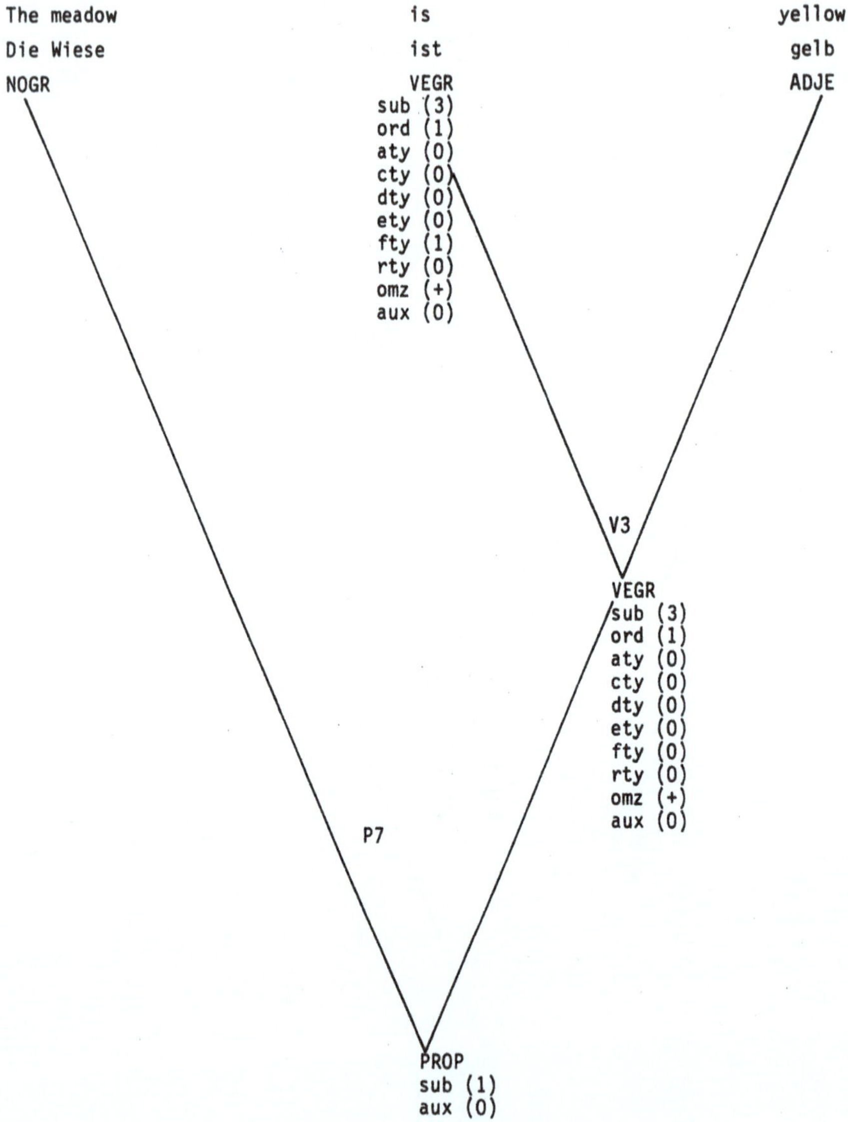
The meadow
Die Wiese
NOGR
is
ist
VEGR
sub (3)
ord (1)
aty (0)
cty (0)
dty (0)
ety (0)
fty (1)
rty (0)
omz (+)
aux (0)
yellow
gelb
ADJE
V3
VEGR
sub (3)
ord (1)
aty (0)
cty (0)
dty (0)
ety (0)
fty (0)
rty (0)
omz (+)
aux (0)
P7
PROP
sub (1)
aux (0)

Example 4a:

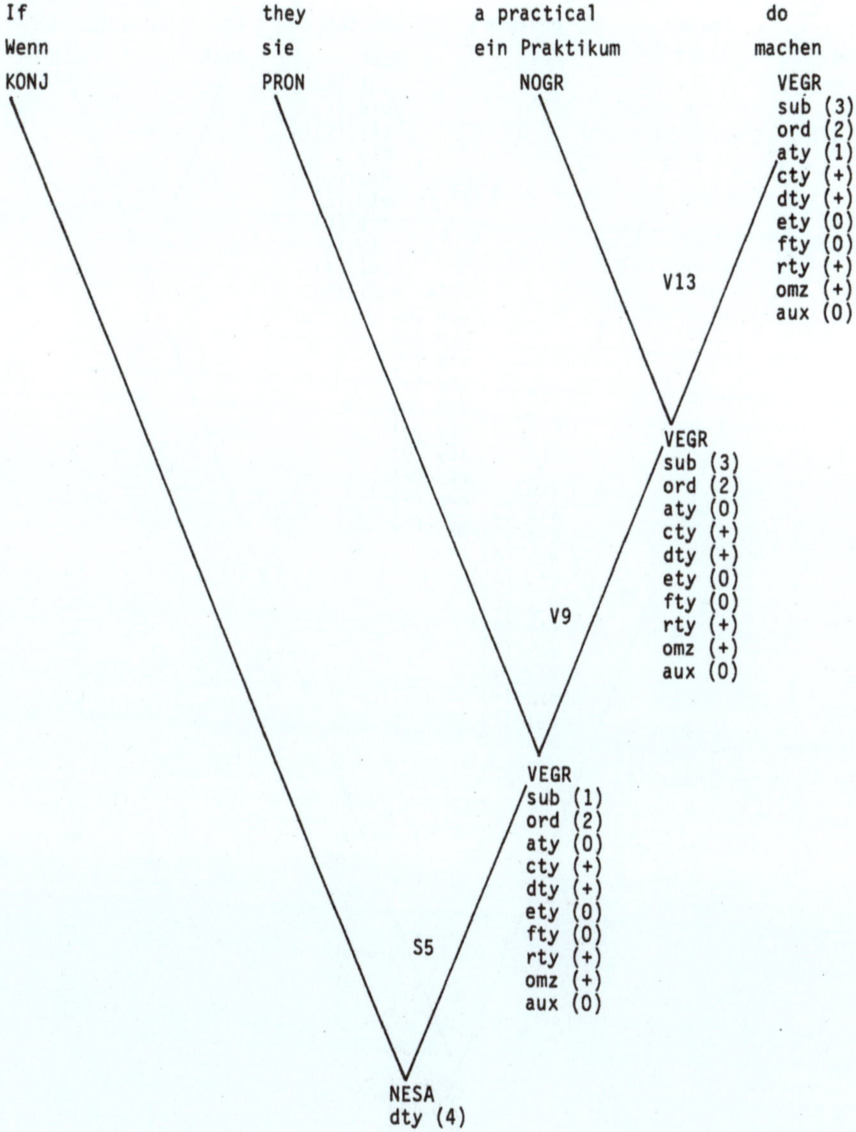
If
Wenn
KONJ
they
sie
PRON
a practical
ein Praktikum
NOGR
do
machen
VEGR
sub (3)
ord (2)
aty (1)
cty (+)
dty (+)
ety (0)
fty (0)
rty (+)
omz (+)
aux (0)
V13
VEGR
sub (3)
ord (2)
aty (0)
cty (+)
dty (+)
ety (0)
fty (0)
rty (+)
omz (+)
aux (0)
V9
VEGR
sub (1)
ord (2)
aty (0)
cty (+)
dty (+)
ety (0)
fty (0)
rty (+)
omz (+)
aux (0)
S5
NESA
dty (4)

Example 5:

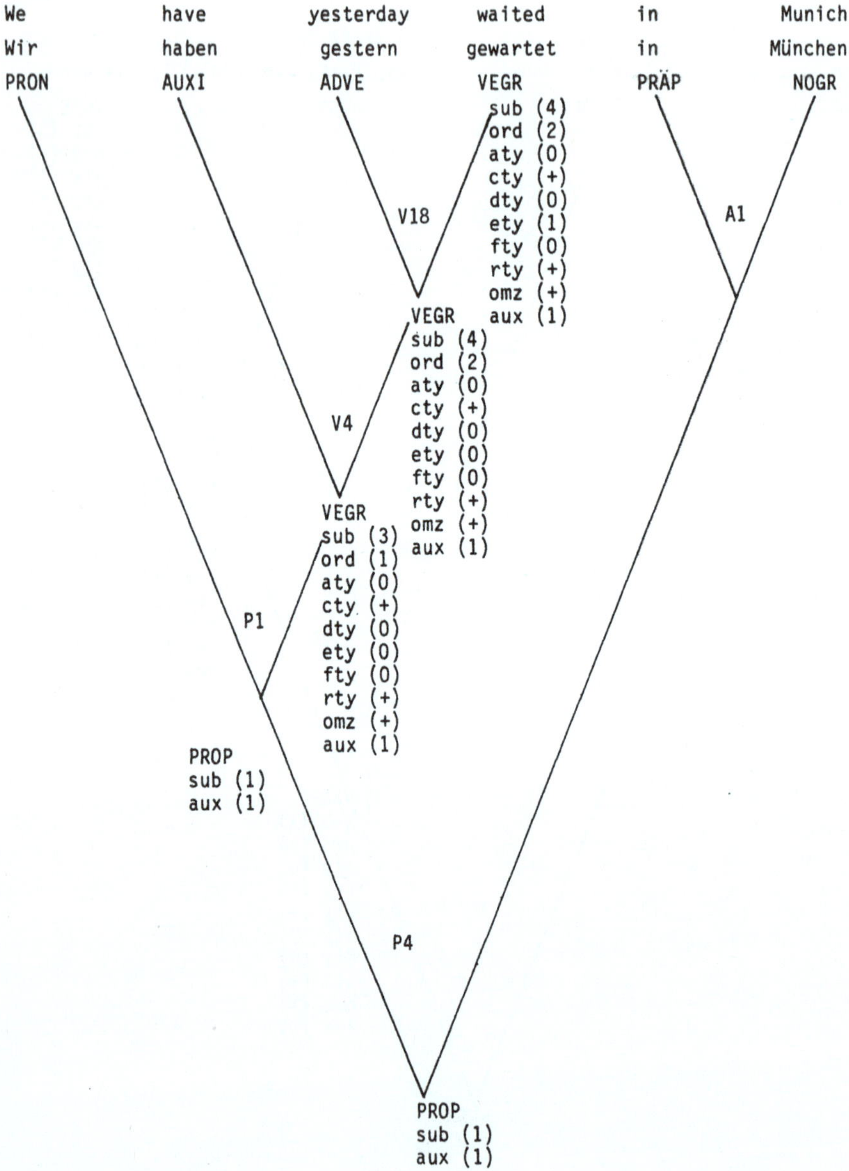
We have yesterday waited in Munich
Wir haben gestern gewartet in München
PRON AUXI ADVE VEGR PRÄP NOGR
sub (4)
ord (2)
aty (0)
cty (+)
dty (0)
ety (1)
fty (0)
rty (+)
omz (+)
aux (1)
V18
A1
VEGR
sub (4)
ord (2)
aty (0)
cty (+)
dty (0)
ety (0)
fty (0)
rty (+)
omz (+)
aux (1)
V4
VEGR
sub (3)
ord (1)
aty (0)
cty (+)
dty (0)
ety (0)
fty (0)
rty (+)
omz (+)
aux (1)
P1
PROP
sub (1)
aux (1)
P4
PROP
sub (1)
aux (1)

Example 6:

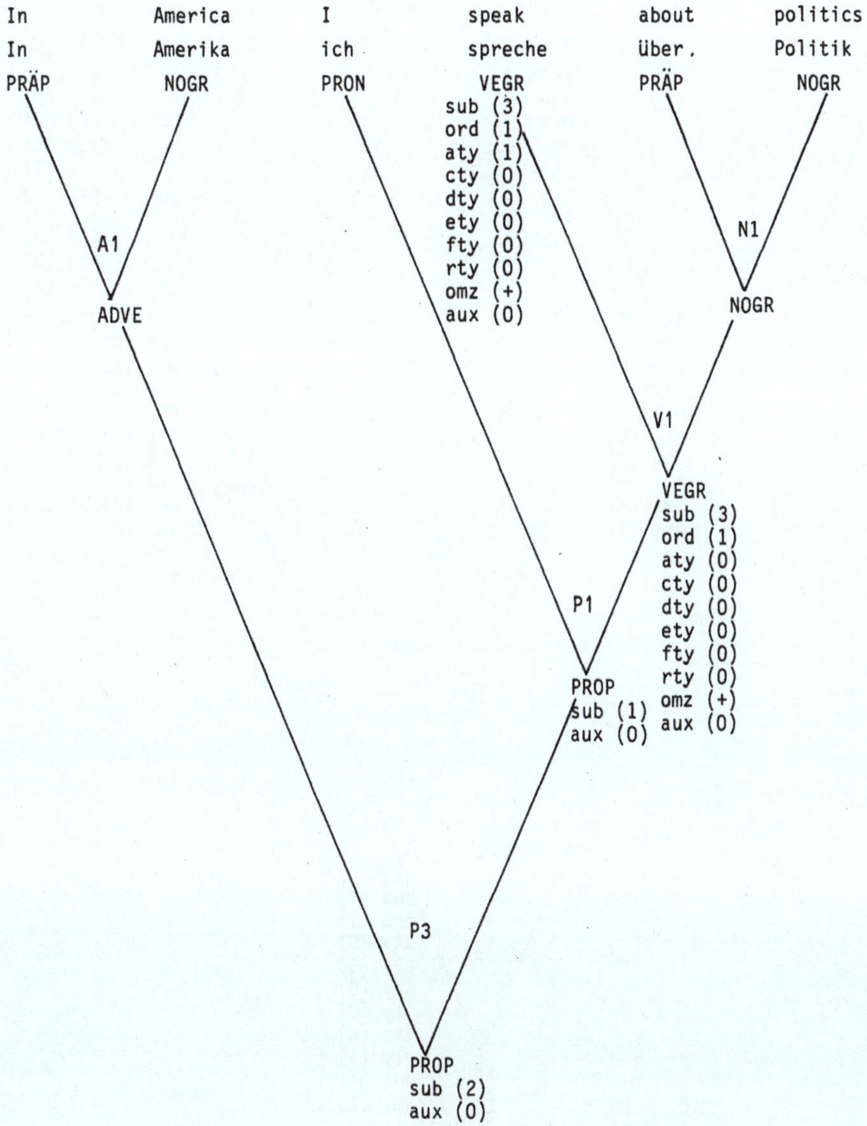
In America I speak about politics
In Amerika ich spreche über. Politik
PRÄP NOGR PRON VEGR PRÄP NOGR
sub (3)
ord (1)
aty (1)
cty (0)
dty (0)
ety (0)
fty (0)
rty (0)
omz (+)
aux (0)
A1
ADVE
N1
NOGR
V1
VEGR
sub (3)
ord (1)
aty (0)
cty (0)
dty (0)
ety (0)
fty (0)
rty (0)
omz (+)
aux (0)
P1
PROP
sub (1)
aux (0)
P3
PROP
sub (2)
aux (0)

Example 7:

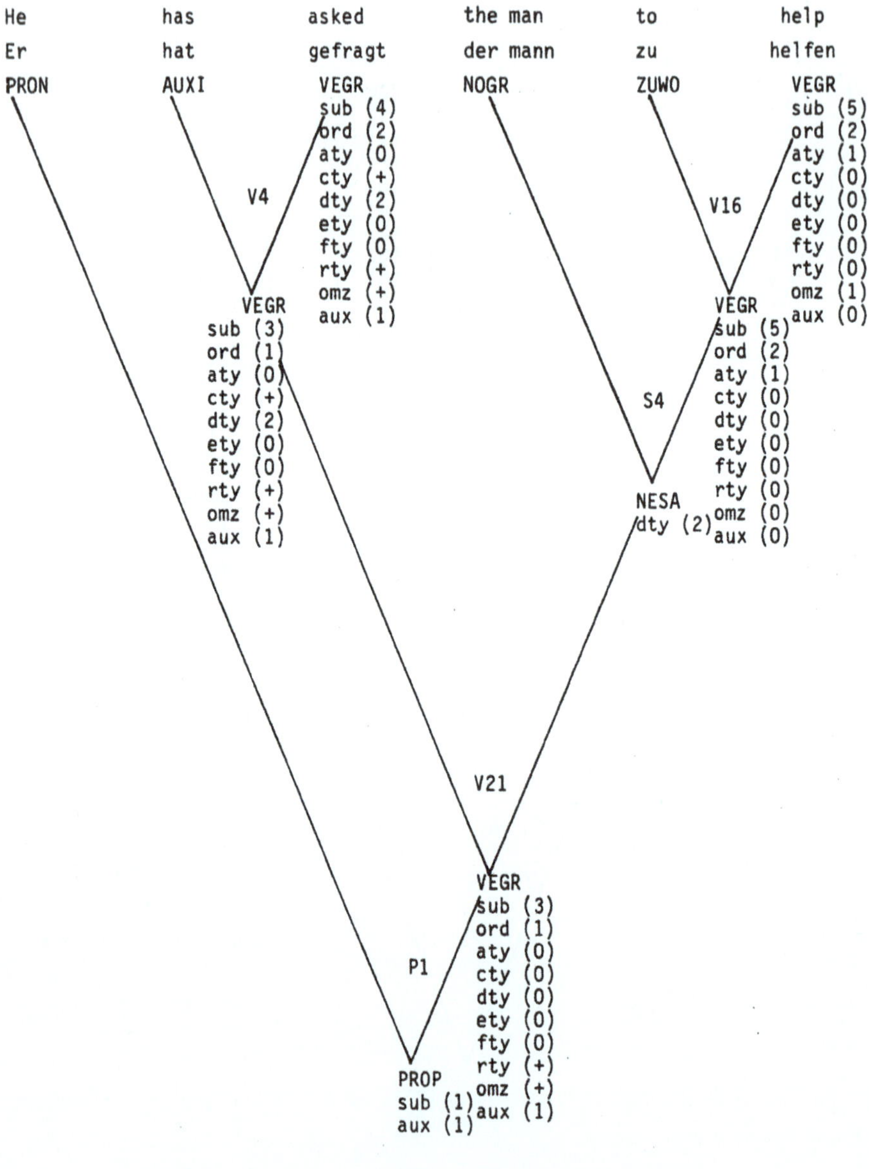
He has asked the man to help
Er hat gefragt der mann zu helfen
PRON
AUXI
VEGR sub (4) ord (2) aty (0) cty (+) dty (2) ety (0) fty (0) rty (+) omz (+) aux (1)
NOGR
ZUWO
VEGR sub (5) ord (2) aty (1) cty (0) dty (0) ety (0) fty (0) rty (0) omz (1) aux (0)
V4
VEGR sub (3) ord (1) aty (0) cty (+) dty (2) ety (0) fty (0) rty (+) omz (+) aux (1)
V16
VEGR sub (5) ord (2) aty (1) cty (0) dty (0) ety (0) fty (0) rty (0) omz (0) aux (0)
S4
NESA dty (2)
V21
VEGR sub (3) ord (1) aty (0) cty (0) dty (0) ety (0) fty (0) rty (+) omz (+) aux (1)
P1
PROP sub (1) aux (1)

Example 8:

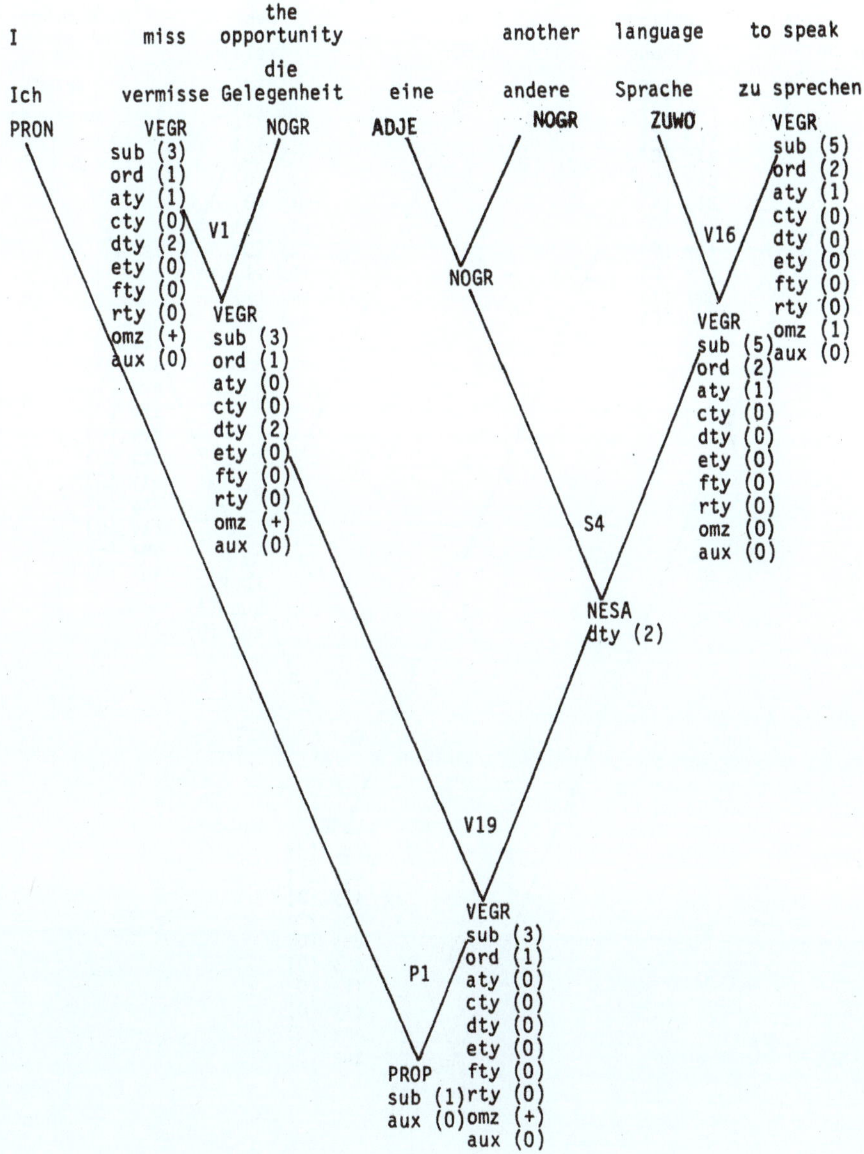
the
I miss opportunity another language to speak
die
Ich vermisse Gelegenheit eine andere Sprache zu sprechen
PRON
VEGR
sub (3)
ord (1)
aty (1)
cty (0)
dty (2)
ety (0)
fty (0)
rty (0)
omz (+)
aux (0)
NOGR
ADJE
NOGR
ZUWO
VEGR
sub (5)
ord (2)
aty (1)
cty (0)
dty (0)
ety (0)
fty (0)
rty (0)
omz (1)
aux (0)
V1
NOGR
V16
VEGR
sub (3)
ord (1)
aty (0)
cty (0)
dty (2)
ety (0)
fty (0)
rty (0)
omz (+)
aux (0)
VEGR
sub (5)
ord (2)
aty (1)
cty (0)
dty (0)
ety (0)
fty (0)
rty (0)
omz (0)
aux (0)
S4
NESA
dty (2)
V19
VEGR
sub (3)
ord (1)
aty (0)
cty (0)
dty (0)
ety (0)
fty (0)
rty (0)
omz (+)
aux (0)
P1
PROP
sub (1)
aux (0)

Example 9:

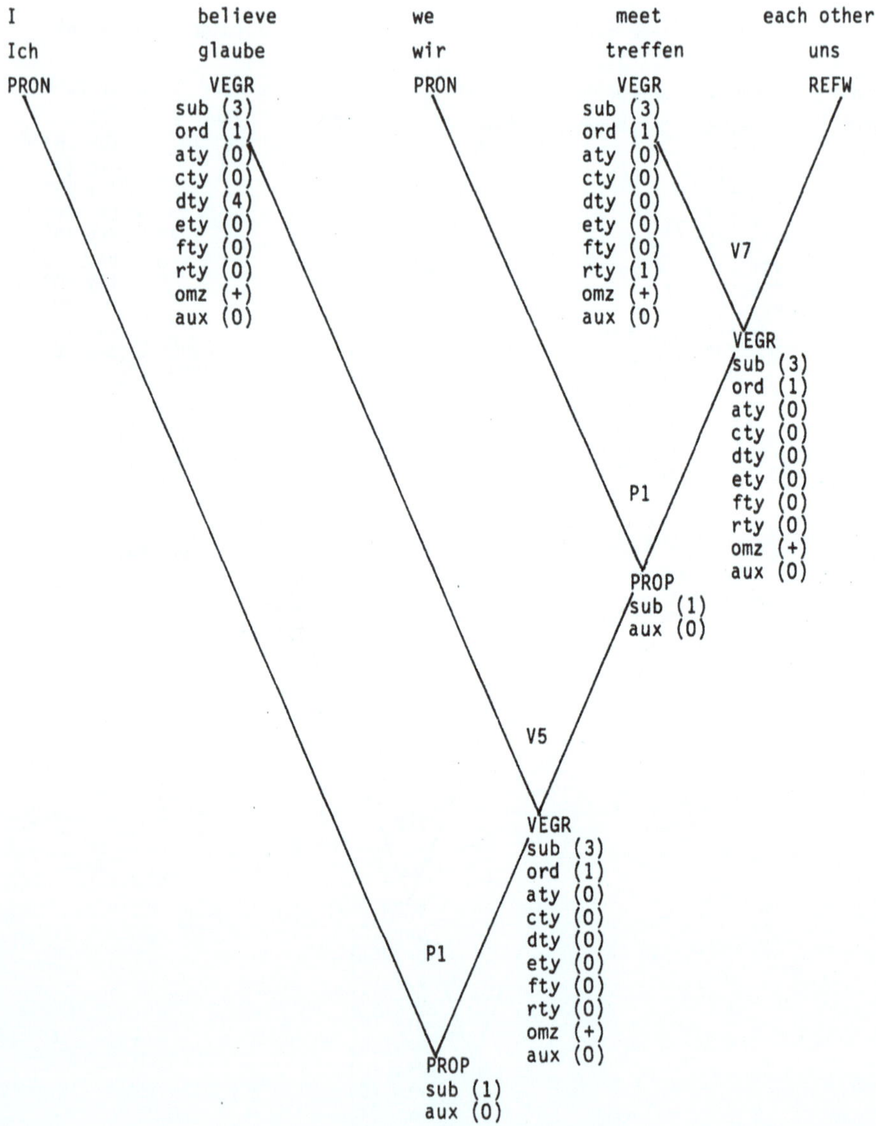
I believe we meet each other
Ich glaube wir treffen uns
PRON
VEGR
sub (3)
ord (1)
aty (0)
cty (0)
dty (4)
ety (0)
fty (0)
rty (0)
omz (+)
aux (0)
PRON
VEGR
sub (3)
ord (1)
aty (0)
cty (0)
dty (0)
ety (0)
fty (0)
rty (1)
omz (+)
aux (0)
REFW
V7
VEGR
sub (3)
ord (1)
aty (0)
cty (0)
dty (0)
ety (0)
fty (0)
rty (0)
omz (+)
aux (0)
P1
PROP
sub (1)
aux (0)
V5
VEGR
sub (3)
ord (1)
aty (0)
cty (0)
dty (0)
ety (0)
fty (0)
rty (0)
omz (+)
aux (0)
P1
PROP
sub (1)
aux (0)

Example 10:

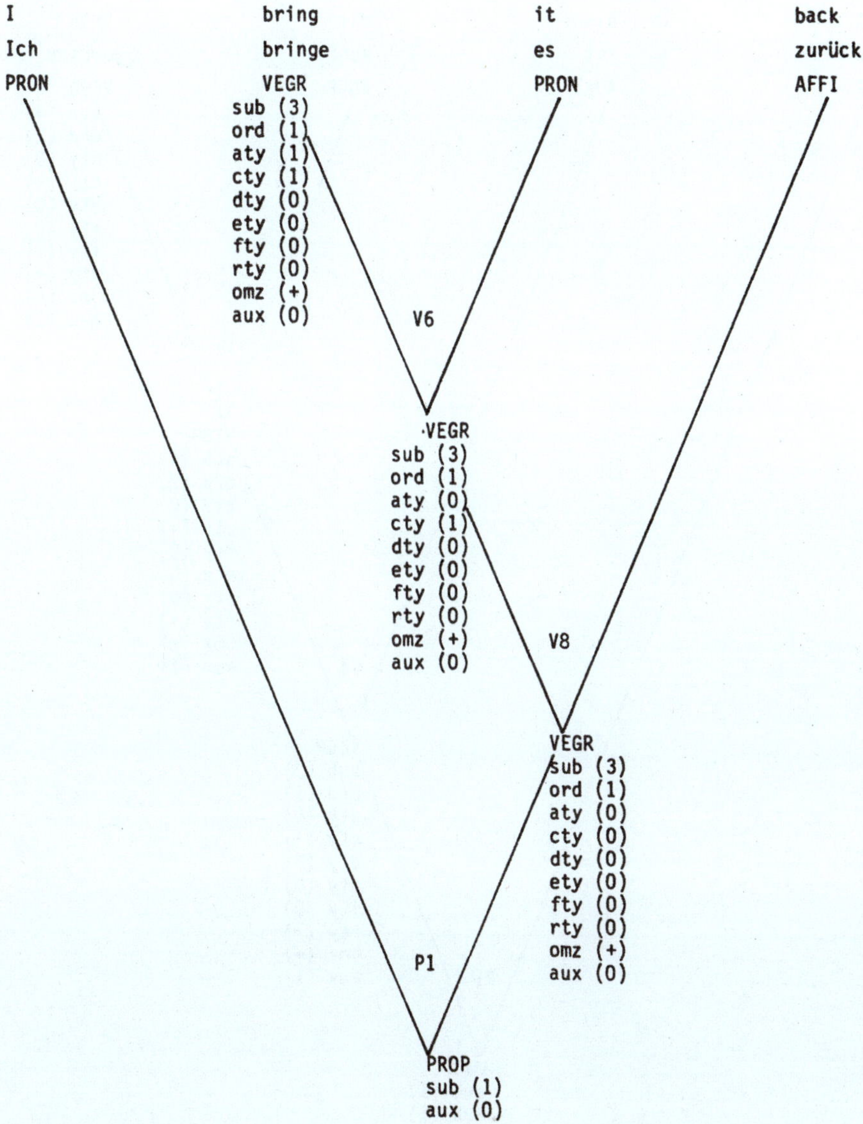
I
Ich
PRON
bring
bringe
VEGR
sub (3)
ord (1)
aty (1)
cty (1)
dty (0)
ety (0)
fty (0)
rty (0)
omz (+)
aux (0)
it
es
PRON
back
zurück
AFFI
V6
VEGR
sub (3)
ord (1)
aty (0)
cty (1)
dty (0)
ety (0)
fty (0)
rty (0)
omz (+)
aux (0)
V8
VEGR
sub (3)
ord (1)
aty (0)
cty (0)
dty (0)
ety (0)
fty (0)
rty (0)
omz (+)
aux (0)
P1
PROP
sub (1)
aux (0)

Example 11:

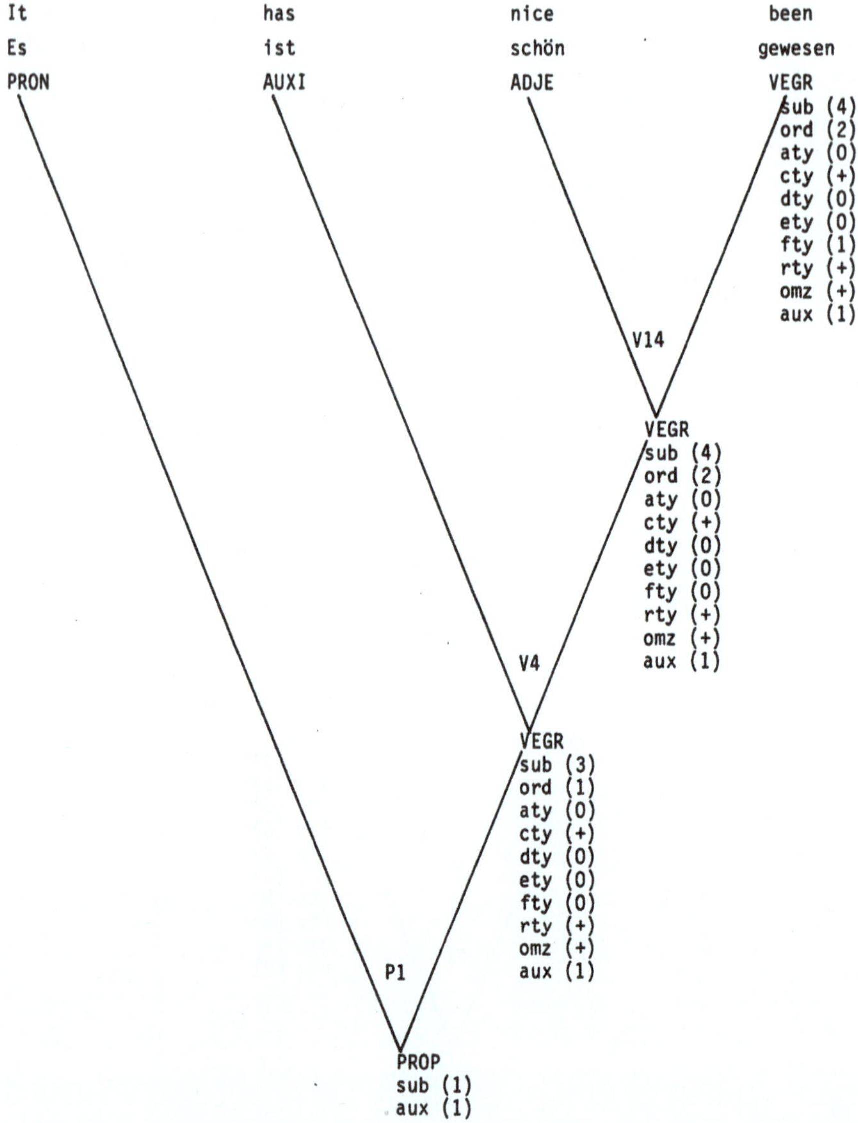
It
has
nice
been
Es
ist
schön
gewesen
PRON
AUXI
ADJE
VEGR
sub (4)
ord (2)
aty (0)
cty (+)
dty (0)
ety (0)
fty (1)
rty (+)
omz (+)
aux (1)
V14
VEGR
sub (4)
ord (2)
aty (0)
cty (+)
dty (0)
ety (0)
fty (0)
rty (+)
omz (+)
aux (1)
V4
VEGR
sub (3)
ord (1)
aty (0)
cty (+)
dty (0)
ety (0)
fty (0)
rty (+)
omz (+)
aux (1)
P1
PROP
sub (1)
aux (1)

Example 12:

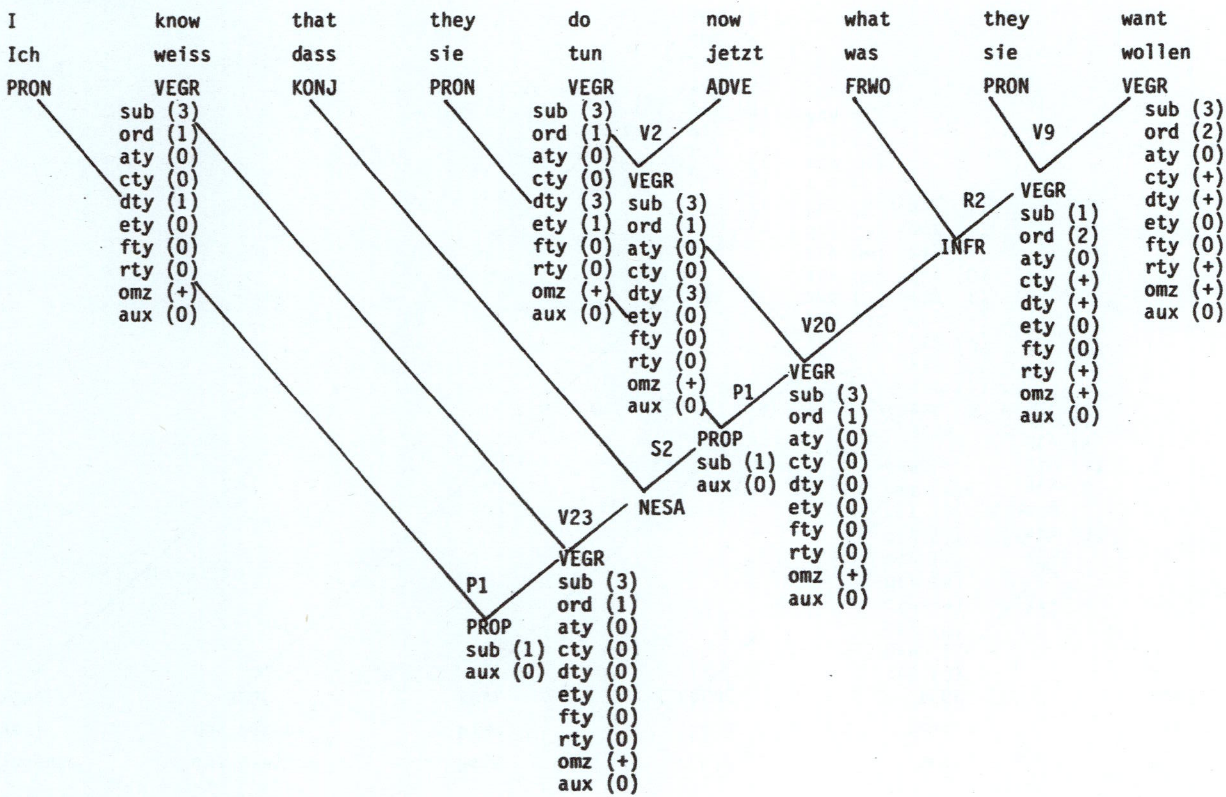
I know that they do now what they want
Ich weiss dass sie tun jetzt was sie wollen
PRON VEGR KONJ PRON VEGR ADVE FRWO PRON VEGR
sub (3) ord (1) aty (0) cty (0) dty (1) ety (0) fty (0) rty (0) omz (+) aux (0)
sub (3) ord (1) aty (0) cty (0) dty (3) ety (1) fty (0) rty (0) omz (+) aux (0)
sub (3) ord (2) aty (0) cty (+) dty (+) ety (0) fty (0) rty (+) omz (+) aux (0)
V2
VEGR
sub (3) ord (1) aty (0) cty (0) dty (3) ety (0) fty (0) rty (0) omz (+) aux (0)
V9
VEGR
sub (1) ord (2) aty (0) cty (+) dty (+) ety (0) fty (0) rty (+) omz (+) aux (0)
R2
INFR
V20
VEGR
sub (3) ord (1) aty (0) cty (0) dty (0) ety (0) fty (0) rty (0) omz (+) aux (0)
P1
PROP
sub (1) aux (0)
S2
NESA
V23
VEGR
sub (3) ord (1) aty (0) cty (0) dty (0) ety (0) fty (0) rty (0) omz (+) aux (0)
P1
PROP
sub (1) aux (0)

Example 13:

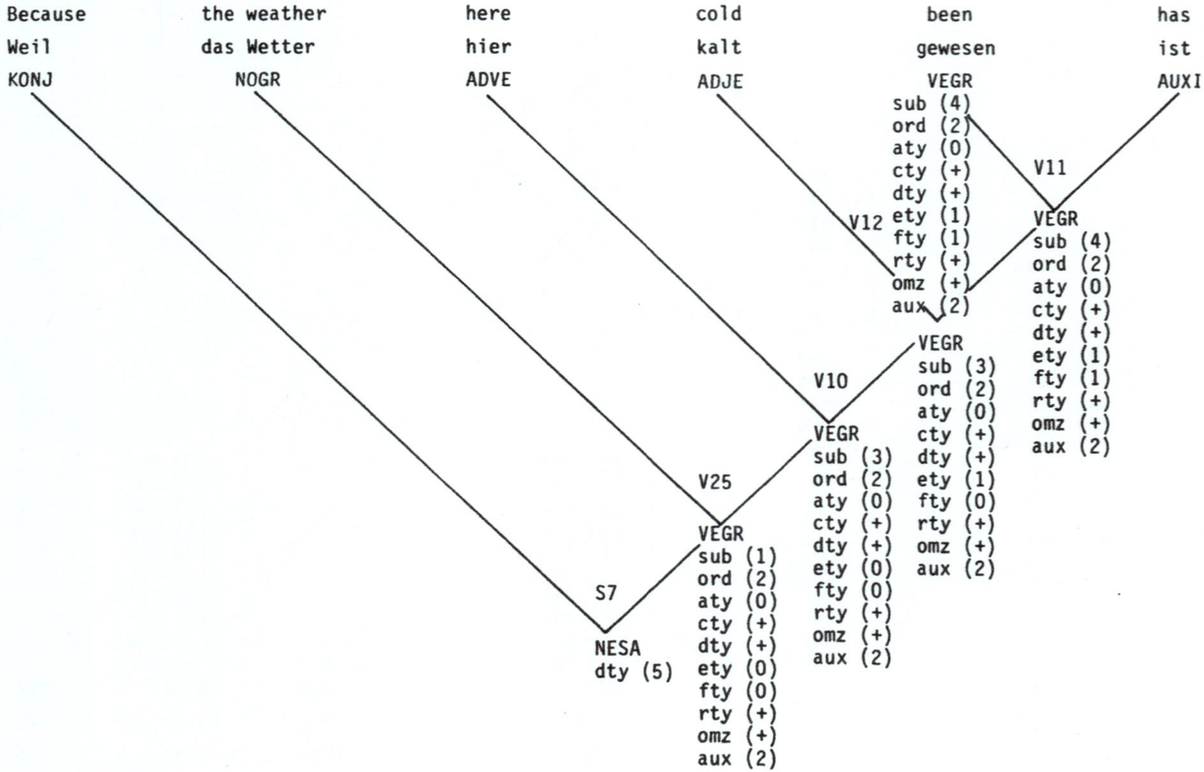
Because
the weather
here
cold
been
has
Weil
das Wetter
hier
kalt
gewesen
ist
KONJ
NOGR
ADVE
ADJE
VEGR
AUXI
sub (4)
ord (2)
aty (0)
cty (+)
dty (+)
ety (1)
fty (1)
rty (+)
omz (+)
aux (2)
V11
VEGR
sub (4)
ord (2)
aty (0)
cty (+)
dty (+)
ety (1)
fty (1)
rty (+)
omz (+)
aux (2)
V12
VEGR
sub (3)
ord (2)
aty (0)
cty (+)
dty (+)
ety (1)
fty (0)
rty (+)
omz (+)
aux (2)
V10
VEGR
sub (3)
ord (2)
aty (0)
cty (+)
dty (+)
ety (0)
fty (0)
rty (+)
omz (+)
aux (2)
V25
VEGR
sub (1)
ord (2)
aty (0)
cty (+)
dty (+)
ety (0)
fty (0)
rty (+)
omz (+)
aux (2)
S7
NESA
dty (5)

Example 14:

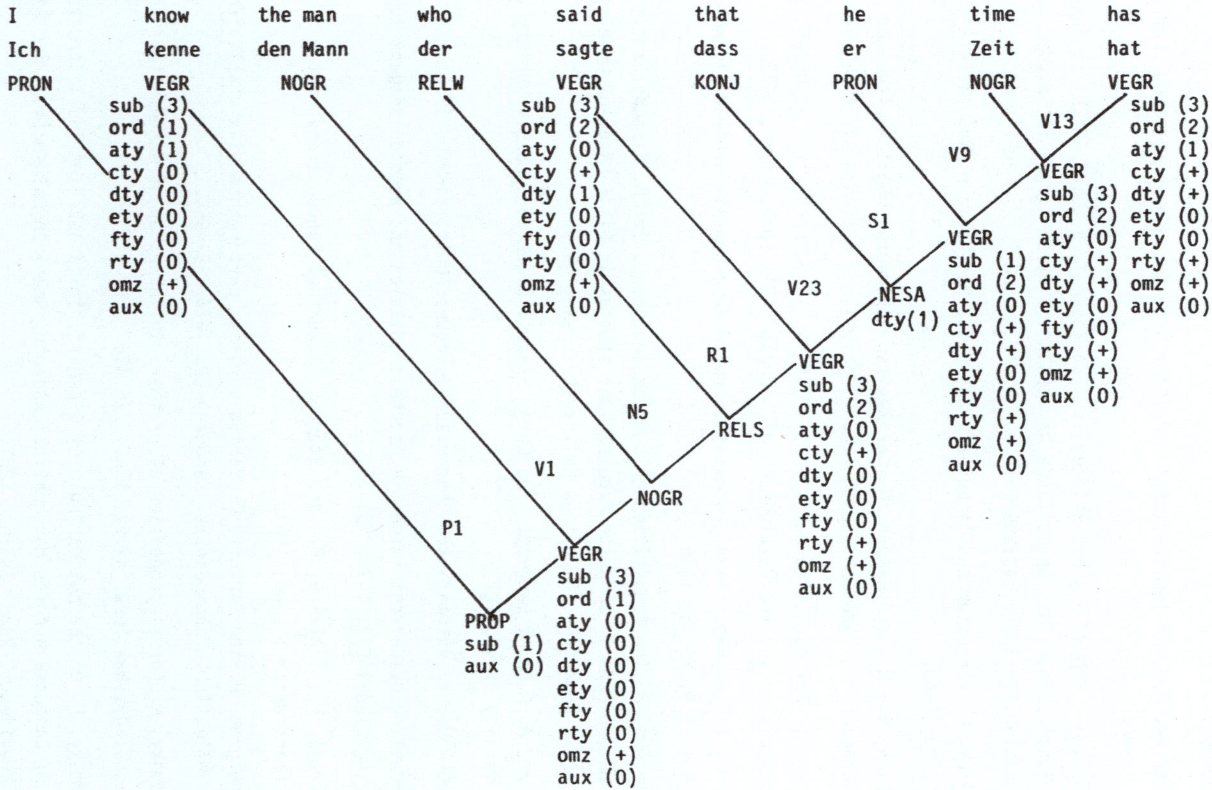
I know the man who said that he time has
Ich kenne den Mann der sagte dass er Zeit hat
PRON VEGR NOGR RELW VEGR KONJ PRON NOGR VEGR
sub (3) ord (1) aty (1) cty (0) dty (0) ety (0) fty (0) rty (0) omz (+) aux (0)
sub (3) ord (2) aty (0) cty (+) dty (1) ety (0) fty (0) rty (0) omz (+) aux (0)
sub (3) ord (2) aty (1) cty (+) dty (+) ety (0) fty (0) rty (+) omz (+) aux (0)
V13
VEGR
sub (3) ord (2) aty (0) cty (+) dty (+) ety (0) fty (0) rty (+) omz (+) aux (0)
V9
VEGR
sub (1) ord (2) aty (0) cty (+) dty (+) ety (0) fty (0) rty (+) omz (+) aux (0)
S1
NESA
dty(1)
V23
VEGR
sub (3) ord (2) aty (0) cty (+) dty (0) ety (0) fty (0) rty (+) omz (+) aux (0)
R1
RELS
N5
NOGR
V1
VEGR
sub (3) ord (1) aty (0) cty (0) dty (0) ety (0) fty (0) rty (0) omz (+) aux (0)
P1
PROP
sub (1) aux (0)

BIBLIOGRAPHY

Andersen, R.W. An implicational model for second language research. Language Learning 28, 1978, 221-282.

Bates, E., McNew, S., Mac Whinney, B., de Vescovi, A., and Smith, S. Functional constraints on sentence processing: A cross-linguistic study. Cognition 11, 1982, 245-299.

Bailey, C. Variation and linguistic analysis. Papiere zur Linguistik 12, 1973, 5-66.

Bausch, K., R., and Kasper, G. Der Zweitspracherwerb: Möglichkeiten und Grenzen der "großen" Hypothesen. Linguistische Berichte 64, 1979, 3-35.

Bever, T. The cognitive basis for linguistic structures. In: J. Hayes (ed.), Cognition and the Development of Language. New York: Wiley, 1970.

Bower, T.G.R. Repetitive processes in child development. Scientific American Vol. 235, No. 5, 1976.

Bowerman, M. The acquisition of complex sentences. In: P. Fletcher and M. Garman (eds.) Language Acquisition: Studies in First Language Development. Cambridge: Cambridge University Press, 1979.

Brown, R. A First Language: The Early Stages. Cambridge, Mass.: Harvard University Press, 1973.

Brockhaus, K. Automatische Obersetzung. Braunschweig: Vieweg, 1971.

Carroll, J.B. Current issues in psycholinguistics and second language teaching. Tesol 5/2, 1971, 101-104.

Carroll, M., Dietrich, R., and Storch, G. Learner Language and Control. Frankfurt/M.: Lang, 1983.

Cedergren, H. and Sankoff, D. Variable rules: performance as a statistical reflection of competence. Language 50, 1974, 333-355.

Chomsky, N. Formal properties of grammar. In: Handbook of Mathematical Psychology. New York: Wiley, 1963, 325-418.

Chomsky, N. On the notion "Rule of Grammar". In: R.Jakobson (ed.) Structure of Language and its Mathematical Aspects. American Mathematical Society. Providence, Rhode Island, 1961.

Chomsky, N. Syntactic Structures. The Hague:Mouton, 1957.

Clahsen, H. and Meisel, J.M. Eine psycholinguistische Rechtfertigung von Wortstellungsregeln. Papiere zur Linguistik 21, 1979, 3-25.

Clark, H. and Clark, E.V. Psychology and Language. New York: Harcourt Brace Jovanovich, 1977.

Corder, S.P. The significance of learner's errors. IRAL 5, 1967, 161-169.

Corder, S.P. Language-learner language: In: J.C. Richards (editor) Understanding Second and Foreign Language Learning. Rowley,Mass.: Newbury House, 1978.

Crystal, D., Fletcher, P. and Garman, M. The Grammatical Analysis of Language Disability. London: Edward Arnold, 1978.

Deutsch, W. (ed.). The Child's Construction of Language. London: Academic Press, 1981.

Dickerson, W.B. The psycholinguistic unity of language learning and language change.Language Learning 26, 1976, 215-231.

Dietrich, R. Generative Linguistik für Psychologen. Stuttgart, 1976.

Dietrich, R., Kaufman, T. and Storch, G. Beobachtungen zum gesteuerten Fremdsprachenerwerb. Linguistische Berichte 64, 1979, 56-81.

Dulay, H. and Burt, M. Natural sequences in child second language acquisition. Language Learning 24, 1974, 37-53.

Felix, S.W. Repetitive orders of acquisition in child language. Lingua 41, 1977, 25-51.

Felix, S.W. (ed.) Second Language Development: Trends and Issues. Tübingen: Günther Narr, 1980.

Felix, S.W. (ed.) Language Development at the Crossroads. Tübingen: Narr, 1983.

Fillmore, L.W. The Second Time Around: Cognitive and Social Strategies in Second Language Acquisition. Ph.D. Dissertation, Stanford, 1976.

Fletcher, P. and Garman, M. (eds.) Language Acquisition: Studies in First Language Development. Cambridge: Cambridge University Press, 1979.

Flores D'Arcais, G.B. Some perceptual determinants of sentence construction. In: G.B. Flores D'Arcais (ed.) Studies in Perception. Milan: Martello-Guinti, 1975.

Flores D'Arcais, G.B. The acquisition of the subordinating constructions in child language. In: R.N. Campbell and P.T. Smith (eds.) Recent Advances in the Psychology of Language. New York: Plenum Press, 1978.

Fodor, J.D. Does performance shape competence? In: H.C. Lonquet-Higgins, J.Lyons and D.E. Broadbent (eds.) The Psychological Mechanisms of Language. London: The Royal Society, 1981.

Fodor, J.A., Bever, T.G. and Garrett, M.F. The Psychology of Language: An Introduction to Psycholinguistics and Generative Grammar. New York: McGraw-Hill, 1974.

Givón, T. On Understanding Grammar. New York: Academic Press, 1979.

Gross, M., and Lentin, A. Introduction to Formal Grammars. Berlin: De Gruyter, 1970.

Hakuta, K. Grammatical description versus configurational arrangement in language acquisition: The case of relative clauses in Japanese. Cognition 9, 1980, 197-236.

Hatch, E.M. (ed.) Second Language Acquisition. Rowley,Mass.: Newbury House, 1978.

Jordens, P. Interlanguage research. Interpretation or explanation. Language Learning 30, 1980, 195-207.

Kahneman, D. Attention and Effort. Englewood Cliffs: Prentice Hall, 1973.

Klein, W. Variation in der Sprache. Ein Verfahren zu ihrer Beschreibung. Kronberg/Ts.: Scriptor-Verlag, 1974.

Klein, W., and Dittmar, N. Developing Grammars. The Acquisition of German Syntax by Foreign Workers. Berlin: Springer, 1979.

Krashen, S.D. A response to McLaughlin, the Monitor Model: some methodological considerations. Language Learning 29,1979, 151-167.

Krashen, S.D. Second Language Acquisition and Second Language Learning. Oxford: Pergamon Press, 1981.

Kratzer, A., Pause, E. and v.Stochow, A. Einführung in Theorie und Anwendung der generativen Syntax. Bd. I u. II. Frankfurt/Main: Athenäum, 1973.

Labov, W. Contraction, deletion and inherent variability of the English copula. Language 45, 1969, 715-762.

Labov, W. and Labot, T. Learning the syntax of questions. In: R.N. Campbell and P.T. Smith (eds.) Recent Advances in the Psychology of Language. New York: Plenum Press, 1978.

Levelt, W.J.M. Formal Grammars in Linguistics and Psycholinguistics. Vol. I and II. The Hague: Mouton, 1974.

Levelt, W.J.M. Skill theory and language teaching.Studies in Second Language Acquisition, Vol. I, No. 1, 1977-53-68.

Lonquet-Higgins, H.C. Procedural theories of linguistic performance. In: H.C. Lonquet-Higgins, J.Lyons and D.E. Broadbent (eds.).The Psychological Mechanisms of Language. London: The Royal Society, 1981.

MacWhinney, B. Levels of syntactic acquisition. In: S. Kuczaj (ed.) Language Development: Syntax and Semantics. Hillsdale, N.J.: Erlbaum, 1982.

Maratsos, M. Children who get worse at understanding the passive: A replication of Bever. Journal of Psycholinguistic Research 3, 1974, 65-74.

McLaughlin, B. The Monitor Model: some methodological considerations. Language Learning 28, 1978, 309-332.

Meisel, J. Der Erwerb des Deutschen durch ausländische Arbeiter - Untersuchungen am Beispiel von Arbertern aus Italien, Spanien und Portugal. Linguistische Berichte 38, 1975, 59-69.

Miller, G.A.,Galanter, E., Pribram, K.H. Plans and Structure of Behaviour. New York: Holt, Rinehart and Winston, 1960.

Ninio, A. and Bruner, J.S. The achievements and antecedents of labelling. Journal of Child Language 5, 1978, 1-15.

Pienemann, M. The second language acquisition of immigrant children. In: S.W. Felix (ed.) Second Language Development. Tübingen: Narr, 1980.

Pienemann, M. Der Zweitspracherwerb ausländischer Arbeiterkinder. Bonn: Bouvier Verlag, 1981.

Richards, J.C. Error Analysis. London, 1974.

Richards, J.C. (ed.) Understanding Second and Foreign Language Learning. Issues and Approaches. Rowley, Mass.: Newbury House, 1978..

Ritchie, W.C. (ed.) Second Language Acquisition Research. Issues and Implications. New York, 1978.

Rosansky, E. Methods and morphemes in second language acquisition research. Language Learning 26, 1976, 409-415.

Salomaa, A. Probabilistic and weighted grammars. In: Information and Control 15, 1969, 529-544.

Sankoff, D. (ed.) Linguistic Variation: Models and Methods. New York: Academic Press, 1978.

Schneider, W. and Shiffrin, R. Controlled and automatic human information processing: I. detection, search and attention. Psychological Review 84, 1977, 1-66.

Selinker, L. Interlanguage. IRAL 10, 1972, 209-231.

Seuren, P.A.M. Internal variability in competence. Linguistische Berichte 77, 1982, 1-31.

Shiffrin, R. and Schneider, W. Controlled and automatic human information processing: II. Perceptual learning, automatic learning and general theory. Psychological Review 84, 1977, 127-190.

Sinclair, H.J. and Bronckart, J. S.V.O.: A linguistic universal? A study of developmental psycholinguistics. Journal of Experimental Child Psychology 14, 1972, 329-348.

Slobin, D.I. The origins of grammatical encoding of events. In: W. Deutsch (ed.) The Child's Construction of Language. London: Academic Press, 1981.

Slobin, D.I. and Bever, T. Children develop canonical sentence schemata. Cognition 12, (3), 1982, 229-265.

Suppes, P. Probabilistic grammars for natural languages. In: D. Davidson and G. Harman (eds.) Semantics of Natural Language. Dordrecht, 1972, 741-762.

Tarone, E., Frauenfelder, V., and Selinker, L. Systematicity/variability and stability/instability in interlanguage systems. In: H.D. Brown (ed.) Papers in Second Language Acquisition. Ann Arbor, 1976.

Tarone, E. Systematicity and attention in interlanguage. Language Learning 32, 1982, 69-84.

Tavakolian, S. (ed.) Linguistic theory and language acquisition. Cambridge, Mass.: MIT Press, 1981.

Wanner, E. and Gleitman, L.P. Language Acquisition: The State of the Art. Cambridge: Cambridge University Press, 1982.

Wode, H. Learning a Second Language: an Integrated View of Language Acquisition. Tübingen: Narr, 1981.

WERKSTATTREIHE DEUTSCH ALS FREMDSPRACHE

Herausgegeben von Rolf Ehnert (Bielefeld)
und
Rolf Klemmt (Jyväskylä)
Donatella Ponti-Dompé (Turin)
Muneshige Hosaka (Mito)

In der Reihe erscheinen Arbeiten, die zwischen Theorie und Praxis, zwischen Grundlagenforschung und der didaktischen Verarbeitung ihrer Texte vermitteln. Dabei ist auch an Unterrichtsmaterialien gedacht. Die Grenze zu Themen aus muttersprachlichen und allgemein fremdsprachlichen Bereichen soll dabei möglichst weit gezogen werden.
Die Bände richten sich an Lehrende und Studierende des Faches Deutsch als Fremdsprache und an Deutschlernende im In- und Ausland.

Band 1 Rolf Ehnert (Hrsg.): Einführung in das Studium des Faches Deutsch als Fremdsprache. 1982.

Band 2 Ewald Reuter: Kommunikation und Institution. Zur Ethnographie des schulischen Alltags. 1982.

Band 3 Jürgen Richter: Handlungsfiguren in kommunikativen Prozessen. Eine konstitutionsanalytische Untersuchung schulischer Kommunikation. 1982.

Band 4 Bodo Scheron/Ursula Scheron: Integration von Gastarbeiterkindern. Theoretische Grundlagen für eine Neuorientierung von Schulorganisation und Pädagogenausbildung für den (Deutsch-) Unterricht und für die außerschulische pädagogische Arbeit mit Ausländerkindern. 1982.

Band 5 Anneliese Sartori Stein: Contrastive Grammar and Exercises English/German. An Exercise Book for Advanced Learners of German. 1983.

Band 6 Rudolf de Cillia/Renate Faistauer/Harald Hanzer/Alfred Knapp/Brigitte Ortner/Danièle Renon: Es darf gesprochen werden . . . Acht Dossiers für den DaF-Unterricht mit Fortgeschrittenen. 1982.

Band 7 Helga Rosenfeld: Erklärungen und Begründungen. Sätze mit kausalem *aus* und *vor* – Eine Korpusanalyse. 1983.

Band 8 Mary Carroll; Rainer Dietrich; Günther Storch: Learner Language and Control. 1983.

Band 9 Brigitte Herlemann/Rüdiger Mellies: Bedeutung – Fremdsprachenerwerb – Interaktion. Fremdsprachenunterricht vor dem Hintergrund von Sprach-/Lernentwicklungsprozessen in Phylo- und Ontogenese. 1983.

Band 10 Mary Carroll: Cyclical Learning Processes in Second Language Production. 1984

Band 11 In Vorbereitung.

Band 12 Arbeitsgruppe Deutsch als Fremdsprache, Bielefeld: Als ausländischer Student an einer deutschen Hochschule. Unterrichtsvorschläge zur ersten Orientierung. 1983.

Stein, Anneliese Sartori

CONTRASTIVE GRAMMAR AND EXERCISES ENGLISH/GERMAN

An Exercise Book for Advanced Learners of German

Frankfurt/M., Berne, 1983. 172 pp.
Werkstattreihe Deutsch als Fremdsprache. Vol. 5
ISBN 3-8204-6265-1 pb. sFr. 44.–

European University Studies: Series 1, German Language and Literature. Vol. 518
ISBN 3-8204-6259-7 pb. sFr. 44.–

The objective of the book is to contrast certain grammatical phenomena in English and German. A cognitive approach is used. Students are presented with the rules of English grammar, then with the German equivalent. The learner then proceeds with exercises. The book focuses on those parts of German grammar that are a particular problem to native speakers of English and usually the source of the most frequent mistakes. The book may be used for self-study since a key is provided. The exercises reflect normal spoken (and written), situational German.
Contents: Incl. The Noun Phrase: articles, determiners, nouns, pronouns – The Adjective – Prepositions and Presspositional Phrase – The Verb and The Verb Phrase: time and tense, mood & modal verbs, voice & stative passive – Conjunctions – Adverbials.

Carroll, Mary / Dietrich, Rainer / Storch, Günther

LEARNER LANGUAGE AND CONTROL

Frankfurt/M., Berne, 1983. 130 pp.
Werkstattreihe Deutsch als Fremdsprache. Vol. 8
ISBN 3-8204-7573-7 pb. sFr. 37.–

European University Studies: Series 1, German Language and Literature. Vol. 637
ISBN 3-8204-7501-X pb. sFr. 37.–

This book presents four closely related reports on the lay-out, data collection and results of a research project on the acquisition of German as a Foreign Language by adult students. A critical description is given of the course of the extensive data collection and the successes and difficulties encountered. This is followed by a theoretical paper in which a model of the production process in second language performance is postulated and discussed. Sections three and four describe analyses of spontaneous self-corrections as evidence of the learner's control of his speech process, which takes into account the influence of individual and linguistic variables.
Contents: Data Collection in the Heidelberg Research Project: Foreign Language Learning at University level – Language Production and Language Acquisition – Self-Corrections: Case Studies of the Speech of Adult Learners of German – Self-Corrections and Learning Focus in Second Language Production.

Verlag Peter Lang Bern · Frankfurt a.M. · New York
Auslieferung: Verlag Peter Lang AG, Jupiterstr. 15, CH-3000 Bern 15
Telefon (0041/31) 32 11 22, Telex verl ch 32 420